ON LOOKING

Also by Lia Purpura

Increase (essays)
Stone Sky Lifting (poems)
The Brighter the Veil (poems)
Poems of Grzegorz Musial (translations)

On Looking

ESSAYS
Lia Purpura

Sarabande  Books
LOUISVILLE, KENTUCKY

Managing Editor
Sarabande Books, Inc.
2234 Dundee Road, Suite 200
Louisville, KY 40205

Library of Congress Cataloging-in-Publication Data

Purpura, Lia.
    On looking : essays / by Lia Purpura. —1st ed.
        p.   cm.
    ISBN-13: 978-1932511-39-0 (pbk. : acid-free paper)
    ISBN-10: 1-932511-39-3 (pbk. : acid-free paper)
    I. Title.
    PS3566.U67 O5 2006
    811'.54—dc22   2005029325

Cover image: *Sonja, 1987.* Photograph by Pierre Radisic. Provided courtesy of the artist.

Cover and text design by Charles Casey Martin

Manufactured in Canada
This book is printed on acid-free paper.

Sarabande Books is a nonprofit literary organization.

The Kentucky Arts Council, the state arts agency, supports Sarabande Books with state tax dollars and federal funding from the National Endowment for the Arts.

For Jed

Every object, well contemplated, creates an organ for its perception.
—Johann Wolfgang von Goethe

*. . . I was also caught by absence
in all its forms.*
—Paul Eluard

CONTENTS

ACKNOWLEDGMENTS

I am grateful to the editors of the following journals in which these essays first appeared:

Agni Magazine: "Glaciology"
Crazyhorse: "Falling Houses: mise-en-scene"; "The Pin"
Ecotone: "The Space Between"
Fourth Genre: "Spires"
Iowa Review: "On Aesthetics"; "Autopsy Report"; "On Not Hurting a Fly: A Memorial"; "The Smallest Woman in the World"; "On Form"
The Journal: "On Invisibility"
Quarterly West: "Coming to See"
Seneca Review: "Red: An Invocation"
Sonora Review: "On Looking Away: A Panoramic"

"Glaciology" appeared in the *2006 Pushcart Prize XXX: Best of the Small Presses.*

For expert reconnaissance, thanks to Kristin Kearby, Ashley Markie-wicz, Jason McCullough, Sarah Sandoski, and John Wixted.

I deeply appreciate the time for work and occasions for solitude made possible by The National Endowment for the Arts, The MacDowell Colony, The Virginia Center for Creative Arts, Thurber House, The Center for Humanities at Loyola College, and my family.

To A. V. Christie, Jed Gaylin, and Maddalena Purpura, my ongoing thanks for your uncompromising honesty and artistry.

Autopsy Report

I wish I understood the beauty
in leaves falling. To whom
are we beautiful
as we go?

—David Ignatow

I shall begin with the chests of drowned men, bound with ropes and diesel-slicked. Their ears sludge-filled. Their legs mud-smeared. Asleep below deck when a freighter hit and the river rose inside their tug. Their lashes white with river silt.

*

I shall stand beside sharp pelvic bones, his mod hip-huggers stretched tightly between them. His ribs like steppes, ice-shelves, sandstone. His wide-open mouth, where a last breath came out. And there at his feet, the stuff of his death: a near-empty bottle of red cough syrup, yellow-labeled and bagged by police.

*

I shall touch, while no one is looking, the perfect cornrows, the jacket's wet collar. Soaked black with blood, his stiffening sleeve. And

1

where the bullets passed neatly through, the pattern when his shirt's uncrumpled: four or five holes like ragged stars, or a child's cut-out snowflake.

*

I shall note the blue earring, a swirled, lapis ball in the old, yellowed man's ear, his underwear yellowed, his sunken face taut. The amber and topaz half-empty fifths his landlord found and gave to police.

*

The twenty-year alcoholic before us, a businessman. All the prescriptions for his hypertension, bagged and unused near his black-socked, gold-toed foot. The first button open on his neat, white shirt and, I shall confirm, the requisite pen in the pocket neatly clamped in.

*

"Oh no," an assistant says. The gospel station's softly on, floaty in its mild joy; it's 7:45 on a rainy Sunday morning and so far I'm the only visitor. Turning briefly to me, he asks, "What did you come here for?"

Then, "Oh no," he says again, "no more eighteen-year-olds," as he stops at the first body, surveying. Soon, the doctors gather in the hall, finish their donuts, scrub, suit up, begin to read from the police reports, the facts meditative as any rote practice, marking and measuring, preparing ritual ground: *The last person to see him alive was his girlfriend. History: bipolar. Suspected: OD, heroin.* "Something too pure is killing these kids in the county," the doctor says. Of the boy's house, the report states "nice," "middle class" and "the deceased's bedroom is cluttered and dirty." Multiple generations at home. Bottle caps with resin in the trash. And here is a silver soup spoon, blue-black from the flame, encrusted where he cooked the stuff, its graceful stem embellished for nothing. As his body is—beautiful now, for nothing. Is olive-skinned, muscled, nicely proportioned. No, I shall say it, is stunning, as it turns to marble before us.

We walk back to the first body, unmingling stories. They divide up the bodies. They take the clothes off.

What I thought before seeing it all: *never again will I know the body as I do now.*
And how, exactly, is that?

Have I thought of the body as sanctuary? A safe, closed place like the ark from which the Torah is taken and laid out on a table to be unscrolled. The two sides parted, opened like, soon I'd know, a rib cage, that a hand with a sharp-tipped pointer might lead the way over, reading toward depth.

Here's the truth: when I first saw the bodies, I laughed out loud. The laugh burst forth, I could not stop it. *Forgive me,* I thought even then, but the scene, the weird gestures looked entirely staged. Such a response is sure measure of expectations; sure proof I held other images dear: shrouds, perhaps? Veils? A pall hanging (and though I've never seen a pall, I know it is "cast over," that it shadows all that it touches). Had I assumed crisp sheets drawn up, as in surgery, to section off an operating theater around the site of death? Had somewhere an ideal been lodged: arms at sides in the position of sleep (not so bird-like, jutting, rigid); faces placid (mouths not slack, not black, empty sockets, dry shafts down, archeological, beckoning, unquiet).

3

Was I awaiting some sign of passage, the strains of ceremony slapping in its wake? (There was the dime the police searched for, evidence caught in the body bag, bright and mud-smeared, I didn't point out. How meager against the royal cats, well-fed and gold-haltered, the canopic jars holding royal organs, the granaries built for the beautiful pharaohs... *leave the dime in, I thought, that the boatman might row him across.*)

Did I expect, finally, the solemnity of procession? Death gowned and dancing, scythe raised and cape blowing, leading the others, at dusk, over a mountain. In silhouette. Fully cinematic.

And now that I've admitted laughing, I shall admit this, more unexpected, still:

When the assistants opened the first body up, what stepped forth, unbidden, was calm.

It was in the assistants' manner of touching their material, their work, that delicacy. The precise, rote gestures feeling space and resistance; adjusting the arc of a blade to the bodies' proportions; cupping and weighing, knowing the slippage, anticipating it; the pressure, the estimate, the sure, careful exchange of hand and knife, the gesture performed so efficiently it looked like habit: easy, inevitable.

The calm came to me while the skin behind the ears and across the base of the skull was cut from its bluish integument. While the scalp was folded up and over the face like a towel, like a compress draped over sore eyes. While the skull was sawed open and a quarter of it lifted away, dust flying, the assistants working without masks. It was calm that came forth while the brain was removed, while the brain, heavy and gray and wet, was fileted with an enormous knife, one hand on top to keep it from jiggling. While the doctor found the ragged lesion in the thalmus and ruled the cause of death hypertension—not alcoholism. Calm, while the brain was slipped into a jar, and the skull refitted, the skin pulled back over to hold it all in again.

I suppose they expected queasiness, fear, short, labored breath—all death's effect. That I'd back away. That after the first, I'd have seen enough. Or the tears that followed fast, after the laughter—for the waste, the fine bones, because these were sons or fathers or would never be fathers—perhaps they expected the tears to return?

But when the bodies were opened up—how can I say this? The opening was familiar. As if I'd known before, this . . . what? Language? Like a dialect spoken only in childhood, for a short time with old-world relatives, and heard again many years later, the gist of it all was sensible. And though I couldn't reply, meanings hung on. A shapeliness of thought was apparent, all inflection and lilt and tonal suggestion.

Nothing was too intimate: not the leaves stuck to the crewman's thigh, and higher up, caught in the leg of his underwear; the captain's red long johns and soaked, muddy sock. Their big stomachs and how reliably strong they still looked. Not the diesel fuel slicking their faces, stinking the building, dizzying us, nor the pale, wrinkled soles of one's foot, water-logged. Not the hair braided by some woman's hands, her knuckles hard against his head. The quarter-sized hole in his twisted, gray sweat sock, sock he pulled on that morning, or afternoon, or whenever he rose while he lived and dressed without a thought to dressing.

Not the dime the police found and bagged. The buckshot pock-marking his face, his young face, the buccal fat still high, rounded and thick. Nothing was unfamiliar in the too-bright room. Not the men's nakedness, although I have never seen twelve men, naked, before me. Not the method by which the paths of bullets were measured: rods of different lengths pushed through each hole—I had to stop counting there were so many—until one came out the other side.

Not the phrase "exit wound."

And though I'd never seen a bullet hole, of course it would be shallow as the tissue underneath swelled uselessly back together. Of course blood pooled each blue-burnt circumference. *Of course*, I remember thinking.

The purpose the work comprised, the *opening*, was familiar.

It was familiar to see the body opened.

Because in giving birth, I knew the body opened beyond itself?

Because I have been opened, enough times now in surgery, once the whole length of me, and there are hundreds of stitches?

Then, when everything was lifted out—the mass of organs held in the arms, a cornucopia of dripping fruits hoisted to the hanging scale—there was the spine. I could look straight through the empty body, and there, as if buried in wet, red earth, there was the white length of spine. Shields of ribs were sawed out and saved to fix back into place. There were the yellow layers of fat, yellow as a cartoon sun, as sweet cream butter, laid thinly on some, in slabs on others. There were the ice-blue casings of large intestines, the small sloshing stomach, transparent, to be drained. The bladder, hidden, but pulled into view for my sake and cupped in hand like a water balloon. Cracks and snappings. The whisking and shushing of knives over skin, a sound like tearing silk. The snipping. The measuring jars filled with cubed liver. The intercostal blood vessel pulled out like a basted hem. The perforating branches of the internal thoracic artery leaving little holes behind in the muscle like a child's lace-up board. The mitral valves sealing like the lids of ice cream cups. And heavy in the doctor's hand, the spleen, shining, as if pulled from a river.

How easily the body opens.

How with difficulty does the mouth in awe, in praise. For there are words I cannot say.

If looking, though, is a practice, a form of attention paid, which is, for many, the essence of prayer, it is the sole practice I had available to me as a child. By seeing I called to things, and in turn, things called me, applied me to their sight and we became each as treasure, startling to one another, and rare. Among my parents' art, their work, I moved in fields of color and gesture, cut parts built to make up wholes: mannequin heads adorned with beads; plaster food so real, so hard the mashed potatoes hurt, and painted sandwiches of sponge grew stiff and scratched. Waxed fibers with feathers twisted into vessels. Lips and mouths and necks of clay were spun and pulled into being in air. With the play of distance, with hues close up, paintings roughened with weaves, softened with water, oil, turpentine, greens, fleshes, families of shapes grew until—better than the bodies of clouds, these forms stayed put—forms spoke, bent toward, nodded so that they came to happen again and again, and I played among them in their sight. And what went on between us was ineffable, untold and this was *the silent part of my life as a child.*

I never thought to say, or call this "God," which even then sounded like shorthand, a refusal to be speechless in the face of occurrences, shapes, gestures happening daily, and daily reconstituting sight. "God," the very attitude of the word—for the lives of words were also palpable to me—was pushy. Impatient. Quantifiable. A call to jettison the issue, the only issue as I understood it: the unknowable certainty of being alive, of being a body untethered from origin, untethered from end, but also so terribly *here.*

And *here*—for we went out to see often—was once constituted by enormous, black, elegaic shapes closed between black gashes or bars. And in the same day, *here* was also curved, colored shapes, airborne and hung from wire, like, ah! muted, lobed organs, so that *here* could be at once a gesture of mourning and a gesture of ease.

I went home and showered, showered and scrubbed in hottest water and threw away the old shoes I'd worn. Later that day, at the grocery store among the other shoppers, I saw all the scalps turned over faces, everyone's face made raw and meatlike, the sleek curves of skulls and bony plates exposed. I saw where to draw the knife down the chest to make the Y that would reveal.

I'd seen how easily we open, our skin not at all the boundary we're convinced of as we bump into each other and excuse ourselves. I'd seen how small a thing gone wrong need be: one sip, just one too many, mere ounces of water in the lungs too much. And the woman in front of me on the check-out line, the pale tendons in her neck, the fibers of muscle wrapping bone below her wool collar, her kidneys backed against my cart—how her spleen, so unexpectedly high in the body, was marked precisely by the orange flower on her sweater! And after seeing the assistants gather the organs up in their arms and arrange them on the aluminum table, after seeing such abundance there—here, too, was abundance: pyramids of lemons, red-netted sacks of oranges and papery onions, bananas fitting curve to curve, the dusty skins of grapes, translucent greens, dark roses, heavy purples.

Then, stepping out into the street with my bags, everything fresh and washed in the cold March rain, there was that scent hanging in the air—a fine film of it lingered, and I knew it to be the milky blueness I saw, just hours ago, cut free and swaying, barest breath and tether. That scrim, an opacity, clung to everyone, though they kept walking to cars, lifting and buckling children in. Packing their trunks, returning their carts. Yes, everything looked as it always had—bright and pearly, lush and arterial after the rain.

On Aesthetics

It is the theory which decides what we can observe.
—Albert Einstein

There was a time, more than ten years ago now, when riding the subway was nearly impossible. Suddenly, for about a week, I could no longer unthinkingly press my body so close to the bodies of others. It was not disgust, nor the summer heat, but a surprising and originless fear. I was managing, but one afternoon on the Uptown Express, slowly, and with great clarity, everyone's face turned ratlike and sharp. Each face was vicious, unpredictable, hungry. And mine was the single soft face looking on, at once too close and isolated from the horror everyone was. By 34th Street, after only a few stops, I had to get off and walk the rest of the way to the Upper West Side where I was staying with my friend.

I returned to normal rather quickly after that incident.

Now that I'm a mother, except for being weird with exhaustion at times, nothing like this has happened since.

Once I did something I can still barely speak of; I know, now, with certainty, it is nothing I-the-mother would ever do again—or rather, fail to do. In a public bathroom at a mall, a little girl was spanked and shaken for not washing her hands before eating. And though I stood near, washing my own hands, I could not dissolve the space between us, the mother, the girl, and me, could not make the girl's hunger mine, move my hand into the crumpled bag of yellow popcorn, take the sheen of fake oily butter onto my fingers, lick the sheen off as she did, nor could I swell with rage like the mother, then break and release order, at any cost, into place. I mean to say I did nothing, said nothing at all. And that it was a failure of heart and imagination.

I left the bathroom feeling so weighted and slow, so stuck at the site of my failure that everywhere I went that day, the bathroom's dank, fake-floral scent, its too-bright air followed and dulled me further.

I now have a child, and because of this, it's assumed in the subtlest ways that being a mother constitutes a certain aesthetic, a frame for observations, a dependable set of responses. For example, if someone sneezes and you, a mother, rummage around and come up with a tissue you're likely to hear "oh, you're always prepared" or even "what a good mother." Actually, I carry tissues because I have allergies and sneeze a lot—just like my father, who never hears about being a good father for handing out Kleenex. He keeps his in a neat little cloth packet, made expressly for that purpose. I suppose I should say, too, that I wad tissues up, before and after use, and they sift to the dark bottom of my knapsack gathering dust. And that I never have enough.

But because I am a mother, I was told a disturbing story. The story belonged to a teenager I knew who recently had a baby. I don't think I reacted as I was supposed to—maybe not enough outrage or pity upfront. Too quietly. And not quickly enough. I watched her face as she told the story; it was round, mild, and smudged by the tasks of the day and I wanted to wipe it. I never thought I would feel that way, though I do now, and often, and for people other than children. I may be over-dramatizing; perhaps I commiserated properly. It certainly wasn't lack of anger that restrained my reaction, but the confusion that always arises when the issue, at heart, has to do with aesthetics.

I know why she wanted to tell me her story: my response would shore up a certainty of hers about mothers, but I'm not sure she was aware of this. I'll tell you the story and some others that gather around it which constitute, really, the whole slippery problem of aesthetics and being a mother.

One afternoon, because she does not have a job (except, of course, for the caretaking) she and the baby were sitting together on the front porch of the place they live when a planet came down, a tiny *planet* she thought, or maybe a jewel, a lit spangle; it was *something* amazing. It came to rest on the baby's head, light as snow but it didn't melt. It traveled, jittery, over the wrinkles on his forehead. She said the circle was M&M-sized. M&Ms were the rule she used. This was the year laser-pointers were all the rage and you could buy them cheap and affix them to anything. Someone had a bead on the boy and held his stillness in place with crosshairs. He must have been an easy mark. I once looked through a gun's scope and knew that crosshairs whittle a viewer's world down to a manageable thumbnail. I remember how purely relaxing it was to see in that way, everything cropped, in focus, contained.

The target shone three concentric rings and made of the flare that could have been pain, a little red spot on the baby's head. The men weren't using the gun as a gun, just as a scope, but I knew, as she herself was learning daily, all it takes is one slip. (And, as if to support this point, I heard later that day from a friend who, distracted by coughing, shot himself in the knee with a nail gun while fixing his fence.)

*

This was the week my son loved the word "knee," and touching mine, his father's, his, spoke the word like an incantation, until it lost sense and began to sound like cheers at a rally. We loved the way an

11

ordinary word collapsed its meaning into pure sound; it made us fall together, laughing.

*

The red lingered on the child's forehead, then moved to the soft spot where the bones had not yet knitted up. As a mother, of course, one reads with both shuddery interest and fear about the fontanel and about being careful, but it always felt remarkably strong when I stroked it. Still, I kept sharp things, heavy things away. A laser, though, will roam anywhere and project the shape of anything at all: Mickey Mouse ears; a glow-red heart over the place a heart should go; a clover-leaf; a lucky 7. Anything with its small heat can dance over the body.

*

I have known the heat of the morning to swell the old wood of stairs, baseboards, molding, and release from within the deep core of a house something of water and dust and age. Even as a child I was pleased by that scent. As it lifted and floated on air, I'd feel I was not alone, that the scent was of my history, there in my grandmother's house, and was conjured anew every day by the heat. I love that smell, still. It catches light and fixes time: early mornings especially, when I stayed at my grandmother's house to get over a cold at my leisure while my parents were working. As I came down the stairs the scent would rise and I'd move through it, toward the couch, to settle in for the day with my fever. My great aunt—it was her house, too— would start cooking, before the pace of the day overwhelmed, the scents would further complicate, and there, my body, warm with its manageable aches, repaired.

*

12

On Looking

Later in the day, after I heard the girl's story, my son and I were playing in an overgrown field. And because I live these days at a crouch, I found a four-leaf clover. I wasn't searching. Nor was I hoping. It was a big one, the size of a quarter, with a shirring of very light, almost white rick-rack along the edge of each leaf. The clover was heavy and moist with dew, the stem a beautifully taut little straw of lighter translucent green. I used to press things like this flat in a book or keep them preserved between two strips of clear tape, but that day I told my son about clovers and luck and then gave it to him to play with however he wanted.

*

The laser on the baby's head was a cherry lozenge, a button, a tack. The color of holly berries, chokeable, dangerous, we keep from our son. It was all a joke. Intended to be, and no, no one was shot. Not the girl who was learning to be a mother, not the baby on whom the light was training.

The laser on the child's head, she learned by their laughter, was "just a joke." And in fact, the men parked at the curb repeated the phrase later to the police. From what the girl said, they were somewhat indignant (though she didn't say it exactly that way) as if she, out of stubborness, refused to admit it was funny. As if she, and not the joke itself, was causing the trouble.

The men in the car parked at the curb laughed at her confusion; in particular how at first, in awe, she followed the light back to the source to be sure it wasn't a holy event she just saw: something alighting. Something bestowing. What they liked especially was the way she jumped up when she noticed the light, and with one arm scrambled the air while screaming and holding the sleeping baby. It was slap-stick funny, lowly as pots and pans clanging down on the head of, say, a bachelor, trying to bake his first cake. And the cake a wedding cake at that! One that, later, would turn out, surprise, to be his! But first, the messy scenes with skidding, twists and turns, a flour-cloud rising, the amusing vertigo that comes from keeping too much in the air at once. They found her thus, heavily up and out of the lawn chair, holding the baby tight, hair a mess, kicking the Coke, crashing in through the meager screen door.

And that's not all; there's more, a kind of backstory: she had been undressed by their sight, which, after it touched the boy's head, traveled up her arm, over her shoulder, and bounced breast to breast. (Maybe they poked one another and said *follow the bouncing ball* and sang a simple, bawdy song. Funny to see her try to brush the beam off like an insect. Perhaps one of them thought she moved delicately then, as if she were a milkmaid, a shepherd girl, wearing a bodice of lace in which some scratchy hay was caught. *Dishabille* might not have occurred, but *kind of messy-pretty?* Maybe. For a moment, maybe. Then he would remember where he was and put the thought out of his head. Because to keep it there would mean he had seen her differently. That she was not exactly funny. And since she was trying to swat her breast and not swat the baby's head, and everything was flying apart, that was enough to think about for now, and he would just laugh along with the rest.)

*

But that's my take. My story, not hers.

*

"Why would they do that?" she asked me.

*

14

On Looking

And although it was insufficient (you'll see why), I did answer. I believe a mother should answer, as best she can, the questions put to her.

*

Once in a park, I stopped to drink from a fountain and there in the cement bowl was a silver dollar. *Lucky!* I thought and bent to pick it up; lovelier still, wet and shining. But it resisted. I pulled and pulled until I heard laughter and realized two older boys were holding the end of some fishing line looped through a tiny hole in the coin. I bent my head and walked away fast, in shame. And then they laughed louder. But when I got home and considered the scene, it *was* kind of funny and I wished I'd thought up the prank. I remember, soon after, looking for books on practical jokes in the library.

*

he he's constructed

When Geppetto made Pinocchio he made a puppet, which of course he could manipulate, make jump at will, and dance. But he didn't want that. He wanted the boy to be real: good but imperfect. I just read the book to a friend's little girl. She liked the lying-and-consequence parts best: the donkey ears, the pole of a nose that a bird, two birds, then a whole flock could perch on. Peck at. Which hurt Pinocchio but didn't stop his being naughty. She liked that, too. It was sad-scary-funny. Or amusing-right-frightening. After we finished the book and were talking, she couldn't say why she liked those moments. And she couldn't decide if it was all right to like them. I said I felt the same way. I said it was complicated. And disappointed in my answer, she went right to bed.

*

15

From their car the men watched a woman move like a puppet, but there was no moral. It was just a great scene. They liked it that way, who, long ago, would have been drunks on a rough bench after days in hot fields, at the foot of the stage of an opera buffa or vaudeville act, any traveling show. Audience, relieved of monotony, for whom banana peel slip-ups are reverie: *better him than me*, better to see *him* go down, land on his ass and turn around steamed, as if to accuse the peel, cracked sidewalk, hole, broken step. Funny, as if it had never happened to them.

And that's the magic of burlesque: you forget, by way of extravagance, that a planet once came to your cheek, that a circle of light, the red eye of a new god traveled to find you at rest and stayed.

You sit back and enjoy the play.

It's someone else's fate on stage: the dumb man's, the sleeping child's, hers.

*

"Why would they do that?" she asked.

*

I was staring out at the yard no one mowed, the baby's clothes on the drying rack, the high, broken curb where the men parked their car. I was thinking: *because they just happened to find it funny. That's why. That's aesthetics. Complex. Unpredictable.*

But I said: *because they're idiots.*

Because, being a mother, I knew what she needed just then.

16

On Form

... It is the forged feature finds me; it is the rehearsal
Of own, of abrupt self there so thrusts on, so throngs the ear...
— Gerard Manley Hopkins, *Henry Purcell*

How does the guy with hooks for arms jerk off?

But it didn't come forth as a joke. Nor was the answer "very carefully."

More powerfully, there was his face, a face used to seeing questions like this in others' faces. How does a face like that look? It didn't shut me down. It didn't slam or ignore or isolate. But he recognized the question (hooks working the receipt into his wallet). He'd heard/seen it all before (outside the store, whoa, he drives a car with those things!). There was a shape to the question and it was a cliché to him. Thus, I felt seen, transparent. Naked. Looked through and turned inside out and found lacking. In imagination. Or just a beginner.

But neither did he see me imagining (the hooks unstrapped, the harness off) his arms on me: small of my back. Back of my neck.

Lifting my hair.

I'm practicing now.

17

Lia Purpura

Someone I know tilts her head to the side when looking hard at another. The gesture always annoyed me and seemed a contrived show of attention. Then I tried it. And it was like voices pouring in; it was like opening the front door and sweeping wide an arm for guests. Like kneeling in front of a child, eye to eye, to ease the confession. Inviting. Hospitable. I didn't know that.

I'll go on then, angled to the pour of these forms.

Though this may seem indecorous.

The hotel manager in Cambridge that afternoon was impatient with me. His name was Khalid. He was bald and had a large, flat forehead that shone. But his forehead was crushed in one spot, like a soda can gets dented. Or a garbage can. And the light lingered there, on the dent, and darkened as I asked—and asked again—for directions to the airport. Someone must run their hand over the dent and smooth it and know the dip of bone and hammock of skin as one knows the contours of a temperamental lock, how to jiggle and fit the key, first one way and then the other, unthinkingly. And though I repeated the words back—Red Line, Green Line, Blue Line, Shuttle—I was really, standing in front of him, jiggling the key. Hand on the tumbler plate, pushing to go in.

My child comes close to touch the imperfections of my face. Touches the flaws because they beckon. The white bumps and red bumps. Small scars. Dark spots. *Counter, original, spare, strange.* He touches because he can, because I allow it, though hiding back there (it's bubbling up, he's capping it, tapping it back down) is this: that thrill without a name. That weird package of love and revulsion, that "glad it's not me" layered over with real tenderness. Some forward sway. Some retraction. And him teetering on the line between.

18

When he does this, all the soft, pink, round things, all the brown, scarred, pitted things that held me as a kid come back. I remember my own secretive glances at the compromised, familiar faces I loved as a child. The tiny, stiff hairs that made nets to catch me. How even as I twisted free, I wanted to be caught.

Here is a man fated to chew as if perpetually working an olive pit out of his mouth. There is a boy who spits when he talks and snuffles and is just too watery to make friends. And with the stem of a dandelion, cut, its bitter milk touched to the tongue, here I am, calling it "milk." Swallowing the bitterness so that an outward sign might match the inner atmosphere I carry with me these last, long days of fall. Swallowing makes me wince and contort. I feel my mouth tighten and take some more in. If it's poison, it's not enough to hurt me, I reason. And anyway, I'm testing. Making tests. Rehearsing ways a face can twist.

I use a mirror for this.

I've been watching her run the bobbing-for-apples booth at the local fall festival with her friends. After long minutes, I draw a horizontal line to see the way the girl would look if her jaw could be fixed, reinvented, if it wasn't so lumpy and overgrown. I draw with a black line, in my head. And then, because I'm at a distance, staring, I squint and hold up a finger to nudge the line of her new jaw into place. But the new line doesn't work. Not at all. The next week, at a restaurant, in a booth across from me, is a younger girl with a half-sagging face and a bulging cheek. I go to work with my tools, sharp scalpel of sight, and pare her back to a simply chubby moon. I tack the sag up by her ear; I fix the slipped mouth. But her face is a soft curve of fine sand, a dune blown to an easy rise. It slips back into place and the fixing is wrong. The swell is like a velvet bag. *What lovely behaviour of silk sack clouds.* Throughout dinner she rested that cheek in her hand, as if she was thinking. Though I'm afraid she was hiding.

"When the eye sees something beautiful, the hand wants to draw it," said Wittgenstein. And DaVinci wrote of the bodies he took apart to study, and to his colleagues inclined to work as he did "... if you should have a love for such things, you might be prevented by loathing ... and if this did not prevent you, perhaps you might not be able to draw so well as is necessary for such a demonstration ... or if you had the skill in drawing, it might not be combined with knowledge of perspective ..."

And so forewarned, I'll try my hand: *Anthony touched my face with his stump.* We were fourteen. Anthony touched my face with his stump. I've said this phrase to myself for years. Sotto voce. Sometimes while walking. I say it in part because I like the beat, the variant anapests that beg another verse or want to break into hymn meter, and in part because that moment so impressed me. I hold the phrase itself up like an object of contemplation. His arm ended just below the elbow, this antic boy with raucous good humor, who played the trumpet and who, himself, called his arm "my stump." The sensation was like nothing else I knew. Not a head, not a nudge. Not a child's knee, not a ball. There was headlong force, texture, heat (this was summer on Long Island) and his unselfconscious desire, which instructed me.

In Botticelli's portrait of St. Sebastian, the one I've looked at most recently in my ongoing study of St. Sebastians, it's the outline of the arrows, the many, whole arrowheads buried beneath the skin, lodged in the flesh and those slight hillocks there, where the tip entered and stuck that holds me. So well-focused and attended, it's more than a detail of the ecstasies of form: light, muscle, shadow. I think it's what Botticelli wanted to paint most of all. The rise of flesh, *stippled, blue-*

bleak; the body so changed and so reshaped, and how to praise that awful beauty—*pied. Plotted. Pierced.* I think this was the task he set himself.

At one time I would go so far as to get out of the tub to better hear my neighbors fighting. I'd reach, dripping and freezing, over the toilet and open the window to listen more closely. I'd wish away the noisy trains coupling down the street. I'd wish away my housemate talking in the driveway below so that I might log new accusations in their falling and rising cadences. I practiced seeing gestures, appointed gestures to their words in the steamy cold. Deformities of anger, gnashing twisted mouths, inner bile stirred and poisoning their postures. I wished them peace, I did. But when they screamed, I felt I could see the corners of mouths pull back. I felt the word "gnashing" freeze a mouth. Eyebrows slant like blades sharply down. They were real gargoyles perched and turned to stone.

All the better for sketching.

Sketching, I consider the line. "These fragments I shore against my ruin"—from a time when so much was felt to be coming apart. But no. My fragments I shore to *reveal* my ruin. And all the similarities my eye is drawn to: flaw. Torque. Skew. I make a little pile by the shore: cracked horseshoe crab, ripped clam, wet ragged wing with feathers. I look because a thing is off, to locate the unlocatable in its features, forged as they are, or blunted, or blown. I look because the counter flashes its surprising grin.

My own deformities, of course, abound, but they are on the inside. I do not mean the flaws of reason, the insufficiencies of heart. I mean my spine fused and fixed in place with metal rods—all inside, except for the eleven months I wore a body cast. And then I was the walking ruin for all to see, the shore to keep in sight while sailing free.

The woman with the half-arm, no, a bit more than half an arm (it stopped below her elbow) stands chatting with her friends waiting for the bus. In a gesture she must have developed long ago, she rolls a magazine into a tube and slips her half-arm into it. How well and how long must the gesture have served, because, really, who hides an arm, a perfectly good arm, in a magazine? Whose but a child's arm could be covered by a magazine, its length or its circumference?

One sees what one expects to see: "a magazine laid over the arm." But because I saw the arm slip in, I see instead her quiet strategy. And what does looking at her, what does knowing that teach me—since all along in here I've been practicing, letting the sight-of work on me. And recording, recording, recording. I am not her parent and so do not feel guilt. I am not her sister and so do not feel that dual reprieve/protectiveness. I call up the warmth of such an arm in my hand (I don't know if she says "stump"), the curve, the balance, its abrupt end, and the ghost of its missing length. I feel, like a child, neither moral nor immoral saying this. I feel many things.

When the eye sees something beautiful the hand wants to draw it. Or here's another way to say it: *a poem should not mean, but be.*

There is not, as many think, any air at all in a jellyfish, just organized cilia and bell muscles, a gelatinous scaffolding for hydrostatic propulsion. These simplest drifters are like bubbles of milky glass—and who doesn't want to see through to a thing's inner workings, the red nerves, and blood and poison with a clear pulse, circulating. And yet one scientist says, "When thinking of jellies we have to suspend our bias towards hard skeletons with thick muscles and dense tissues." He means in order to see their particular beauty, to see *them*, we have to suspend our fear. We have to love contraction. Filtration. The word "gelatinous," too. The words "scull" and "buoyancy" are easy. We have to suspend "mucus web." And realize that their bio-luminescence, which is a show to see at night, is used to confuse and startle prey. You can look right through them. As if into a lit front room when it's night outside.

Of course, we peer into houses at night not because they're beautiful, but because we want to see what's going on in there— illuminated, partial, and beckoning.

I've carried this image for a long time now: the port-wine birthmark on the girl's pale face. All that summer at the beach, the mark was like a harbor, or what I knew of the shore, growing up near the ocean as I did. Tidal, it crept up near her eye and stayed like a dampness. I felt I was supposed to separate that color—velvety, royal, berrylike—from its place: her face, where it shouldn't be. But I could not get the color to be unlovely. And I could not remove the mark from her face.

Magda, who worked at my favorite lunch counter in Warsaw, had the lovely, plain face of a farm girl. When she laughed, her white teeth shone and the scar in the middle of her chin puckered. And when she looked past me, into the distance, one eye rolled to the side. Her left eye was fixed in place during our conversations as she ladled out the borscht with beans I ordered every day. And every day, I'd wait to see it slip away—the whiteness, the angle, the variation: the hand wants to draw it. If that which is beautiful is balanced and symmetrical, a "pleasing unity," then the unbeautiful's more a form of interruption— like a gasp. A catch in breath. The unbeautiful's a form made of interruptions—a rough hand passed over wool's nap, snagging. And passed over again and again for the snag. It's a moment that catches your attention. It's a moment into which you fall, as when on a crowded bus, hot crowded subway, you forget yourself and enter some other, less populated world by an unexpected door: a woman's earlobe, deeply notched; the close back of a man's neck, oily and creased; a girl's cracked lip; a freckle; a boil; a split thumbnail with its crescent of dirt, next to which your own nail rests on the cool, aluminum pole.

Recurrences/Concurrences

Conditions are present.

Frost on the bathroom window this morning burgeons and twines in winged fleurs-de-lis. Astonishing frost on this, the same morning I discover my mother's old cigarette case: the same, precise blooms but in silver-etched motion. How the mind of frost, the form reaches out, draws its heirs close: from anywhere, cracked riverbeds and leaf-veins in sun. From a few blocks away, wrought-iron fish on the Roland Park schoolyard fence. From childhood, Dead Man's Fingers, *Codium fragile*, common seaweed, washed up on any Long Island beach.

And this afternoon, sitting down to work, a plastic bag catches in a bare tree and stays. I can see it from up here, from my second floor window. Up here, it's Baltimore. The middle of winter. But I know this thing, puffed full of air, the four corners taut, is a swollen egg case, a skate's or a ray's: *Mermaid's Purse* we'd find at low tide, shining and black and tangled on shore.

Forms everywhere watch and align.

25

Lia Purpura

I once had a friend. He had been teaching a long time when I was just starting. He liked telling his students he'd seen them before. In another life, at another school, the same hairline, the same kid brother back home in eighth grade. In class, he gave them obituaries to read. And though we're no longer close, here is consolation: I still believe in what he was up to: seeing if he could make them dizzy. Suggesting they write their way into or out of the disquieting facts he offered up. Offering the chance to find themselves breathless, to consider themselves a point on a circle falling and rising, falling/drawn up, as the wheel moved, moves, is moving relentlessly on. He wanted them to feel *conveyor* beneath their feet, when all along they'd assumed they were walking. To consider they might, somehow, for another, be a mark and a measure of vastness. A site.

As he was for me.

What do you see? What aligns? he's still asking.

Fronds of frost. Crystallized leaves. Ironwork, sterling, the form recurring. In Belgian lace, threaded with light. In Russian tea glasses, the filigree heated by steaming, sweet amber. In coral arms. In branching veins.

In this way I begin to speak to him. Slant and sidelong.

A path through this thinking is clearing. Stay with me. Events will fit themselves to themselves. Stitch along and proceed.

Without the site of this essay, these moments are nowhere. And Reader, without you, this reflection on things remaking themselves—fern into ice, ice into sea plant, faces and lives over time—is unseen.

Stay with me.

*

On Looking

What about this: these moments of recurrence/concurrence are not messages fluttering toward, bearing secrets, but stories in which we are part of the telling. We are, for a spell, of the path where shape forms, where flux assembles, briefly, a center.

And there are so many centers.

What does this sound like:

Where I held my finger to the window and warmed a small circle in frost this morning, a new flower has grown. The new flower began in the shape of a star. *Codium fragile*. Silver-leaved. I am only writing what is true—true to form—when I say the flower, whose fronds are in motion, grew from a star. To say every scrap of matter bears a trace of the beginning of the universe, that a star lives in our blood, a star with its fingers in the riverbed of our bloodstream, tributaries, filigree, silver-etched, is a fern, an ice crystal, to say that the star's disappearance, ongoing, is what we see looking up at night—sounds unbelievable.

This sounds unbelievable.

But sitting down to this work, this work, too, seems unlikely: that particulars mingle, particulars assert, conspire, assemble. That what I didn't know I knew was *somewhere*...waters be gathered, waters bring forth...and how, what seems in the end like intention, arrives only piecemeal. How what seems in the end *inevitable*, is a trail of particulars finding each other.

Of course, I could say *I won't write about my old friend*. And, to be honest, I'd rather not, since I still feel regret and sadness about that loss. But things about him assert here as subject. The obituaries (you'll see). The dizziness. His belief in the uneasy matter of chaos. It's all, here, important. All-of-a-piece. These lightest of strands, moments, memories unbury. Forms align in each others' presence.

It's the noticing that cracks us open, lets something in.

Shows we're in use.

Uses us.

Right now. Right this minute.

*

So often these days my son—who is busy getting the basics down—
asks "why?" and "is that the rule?" Here's what I think to myself
(though I sometimes impatiently say "*Yes*, it's the *rule*"): I make the rule
up, moment to moment. I mean, the moment conjures the rule.

Like this:

the surface temperature must drop below freezing, must drop
below dew point; the dew point must hover, and then frost will form.

By reaching into the nothing there.

The emptiness waits to crystallize, to filigree.

It's the same emptiness the clam steps into, stretches its single,
pink, muscular foot toward. The clam stirs the water. Hits something
hard: retracts/waits/proceeds. Foot out and in, it stitches along.

A few days after surgery, as I write this, recovering, I am thinking
about stitches. Behind bare trees is the hard blue sky. The snow-glare
reflects and it's very bright. Three planes mark white, discrete lines
in the sky. I look away for what seems just a moment and when I turn
back, the jet trails are gone. Wholly dissolved and the blue is all
healed. Just like that.

Just *like*.

I saw once a reenactment of an old British parlor game, *Similes*.
The host goes around the circle asking "Slippery as a _____,"
"Sharp as a _____," and the players fill in the correct word—that
is, the known, the agreed-upon. As a *fish*. As a *tack*. It's a game for
those who like playing by rules, slipping into, not standing back from.
Those wanting a clean end. As a fish! As a tack! No watching for
forms, no rogue search here, but much good citizenry all around.
Bright as a _____ ? *Star*-bright, of course. Not *bright as frost. Fern-*

bright. Fern-dark. Sea-fern green. Fern-frosted. In the fern-frosted silence. The dead man's fingers frosted over. Ice-sharp. The stitched sky. A filigree purse.

I just came upon this, in a book I'm reading: "When a man dies, his secrets bond like crystals, like frost on a window. His last breath obscures the glass."

The frost. The crystals. A Dead Man with secrets moving like fingers: it's all here. All there. Here and there, piling up. What does my friend want his students to say, what does he want them to stumble into, considering those obituaries? "Nothing in particular," he'd answer, meaning "I have no plan." No one thing in mind. Only for them to skid to a halt, to go breathlessly forth, for here is their chance to see: the patterns keep coming, all the lives theirs resemble—in the newspaper photo, the deceased at age twenty, the jaunty tilt of that head so like the tilt of their own. That they share the same name, the same birthday and interests. That the most basic, seismic events daily converge and include us.

Daily Seismics

A few days ago, six o'clock at night: I am cutting strawberries and thinking of my father. I call him up. His hand is on the phone, ready to call me. It is six o'clock. He is cutting strawberries.

A few days ago, at dinner, I suggest that my friend read *The Gift* by Lewis Hyde. I try my best to say why, and why now in her life she should read it, try to sum it all up as an antidote to troubling times. Hope I've done a convincing job. I feel very strongly about this, though I wonder if I've been prescriptive, annoying. When we finish our meal, I drive home and park on the street. I pull up behind a car whose license plate reads "HYDE."

And yesterday morning, settling in with the dictionary to find some new words, I land first on *hagioscope*: a small opening in the interior wall of a church designed so those in the transept can see the altar. I write the word down and its definition. Later in the day, at the dentist's office, I open a magazine and there, right there, is a review of a book called *Hagioscope*.

Each time, the sensation of being slapped on the back, of some joke in the air: *don't say I never gave you nothin'*.

Something's near coughing from laughing so hard.

The jet trail's white stitches. The white haze of recovery. After my first surgery, years ago, *those* stitches, in black, the whole length of my spine. And now, lying here, I'm remembering that recovery room and in the bed next to me, the ballet star, also thirteen, who would never again dance, the scoliosis twisting her spine, and the surgery, a fusion like mine, inevitable. How, clutching her parents, she sobbed for days, "What will I do? What will I do?" In bed, today, thinking of her, I pick up the paper, flip to the obituaries: *Tanaquil Le Clercq, 71, the ballerina who dazzled the world in the 1940s and '50s before her career was cut short by paralytic polio*...and how she went on, as another person. Choreographer. Teacher. Author.

*

In the portrait by John Singer Sargent, "Lady Agnew, 1892," the subject looks so startlingly like me that others over the years have sent postcards and reproductions noting this. Lady Agnew sits languidly in a wing chair, in a light purple dress, worn as easily as a breath. I wear nothing that easily. And though there is much unlike me here—her slightly skewed gaze, one eye looking up, the other off to her right, the longer, narrower waist, and gold worn at the wrist—more stubbornly, potently, I am there: in the widow's peak, and dark, arched eyebrows, one steeper than the other, the body held firmly against the chair's frame, face intent, its jumpiness contained. The long sleeves pushed up past the elbows: I do that, assuming the day will take work. I see in her how I try, and fail, to hide my impatience. An art historian calls her "elegantly assured," her expression "tantalizingly ambivalent," notes that her face "seems all possibility." In her lap she holds the tight bud of a white rose, which could be crumpled paper or a handkerchief at first—something beautiful and useful, or used. She seems both resistant and engaging at once. The sash at her waist is tied tightly, and yet an armful of purple silk falls in a bright sheen over her thigh and down in a broad heap of soft folds, like a bouquet of lilies, upended. Its studied drape is made to look casual. Her hair is pulled back but rises above her forehead and gathers in a shadow at the back of her neck. I look hard at the painting, as if at a mirror, waiting for it to reveal me more fully to myself. Where her hair and the background darken together, her left ear is obscured, so the viewer's eye slides easily down, over the flushed ridge of collarbone along a gold chain to a pendant. And there, reduced and contained, the icy blues and plums collect.

At the pendant's center is a stirring of light, a reflection shaped like a heart, or a keyhole. A reflection shaped like a snowy owl, its tiny wings folded and head tucked in.

A snowy owl that is also a heart, if you squint a bit. That is also a keyhole, if you look at it sidelong. If you believe that, off to the side, so many things hover, and wait to come in.

Brown

I n this body of brown, in this pile of sticks come upon on my walk, are two black, stripped-bare ones, and a snarl of red vines mingling in, crawling up, or of a mind to. And there's some yellow gone past its bearings, all underside and protected curl. There's a yellow sanctified. An escharotic. Hints and tangles. Yes, brown's a combustion, moving and reckless. Brown's a lobster of moss and bark. (Remember these tender antennae in air, probing for signals and knowing *don't touch rock, anemone, star, but sift for a radiant depth, bent and scattered.*)

And, too, with a stick in its mouth of sticks, joy in its face as it comes from the tangle, brown's a dog, straight-on, (mid-run, it must be) eyes shadowed and nose, that brightness, a wetness. Its tail a live coil diving back in. A dog decohering. *Fascicle. Fascia.* Driving toward *fascis: a bundle.*

Then it all pares away.

Brown junks and darkens upon itself.

Lia Purpura

Starts over again the next day.

I've always disliked, in the name of precision, and for their resolve, landmarks.

Brown meanders.

There's that lobster again, right here, the size of, oh ten or twelve dog heads—one of which is all I can make of this form emerging from its tender surround, the scrawl of it, the matter crisscrossing, those buckled, stray, wiry shoots shooting out. Over grainy, bright eskers. Honeycomb rotars. Rump curves and cochlear swirls pricked up. Black eyes on stems. Haunches ruffled in wind.

A lobster-dog.

Which if I had to look for, en route, means I'd find a pile of sticks, and turn left, and keep going, since such an attraction cannot be arranged.

Sugar Eggs: A Reverie

For years I have collected the occasions for this space—perhaps, in part, for just this occasion, which I do not expect will finalize the subject in any way. The space I'm speaking of has its perfections—though you'll see how I'll have to name it, and name it again to try to get at it. (A list, after all, is an incantation. In a list of likenesses, each element, each peculiarity gathers, leans into and flicks on the light in the room of the next one. The elements loop and knot forth like a net, band as a colony of frost or coral reaching, suggesting not so much a progression as a collective tendency toward. And taken together, the elements offer the assurance of a stance: here is a way to speak of this lightest, barely perceptible—in this case—space. From here I can count and collect that which stirs, and has always stirred me.)

A list inches one closer. Hints along.

So. This space has something to do with the distance between the eye and the rioting, tumbling, crashing stuff a kaleidoscope's mirrors tilt and multiply (glycerin, spangles, dichroic glass)—although a kaleido-scope's stillness is interrupted, is meant to be interrupted by the novelty of combinations, a parade of rays and tatters, a wild field in storm.

The space is informed by the provocations of the hologram which show, by way of shadows and intensities of light emulsified, a tricky, flirting depth. And though you'd think it would be illustrated thus, the space I'm talking about is not well represented by the golden mean, those ever-increasing, spiral-sectioned rooms contained in the nautilus's shell—each chamber's archway carefully built and then, as Oliver Wendell Holmes wrote in his poem, "The Chambered Nautilus"—"its irised ceiling rent, its sunless crypt unsealed." "Chamber" is certainly part of it. And somehow even "crypt." But my space is more forestine: "like a green tunnel leading from the noise of summer into the silence." It is more companionable, a space whose "quietness comes from the silence that is enclosed within it."

I have been considering this space since I was a child and its particular atmosphere is best illustrated by—and I offer no apologies, mean not the least bit of kitschy irony here—sugar Easter eggs. The space is contained between the egg's two crystallized halves, sugar-soldered around the middle, so the hollow inside shows (dimly through the sugar-domed sky) a scene: glazed disk of blue pond, whipped peaks of snowy mountain, hard yellow ducks with black-dot eyes and scalloped, grainy sugar bushes. Distant, rick-rack sugar trees. Pointy, rainbow flower-dots. The space is a privacy into which, as a child, I imagined, not my body but myself, eye to the window at the egg's pointed end, the dim, egg-shaped world before me.

Recently I learned that Mitzi Purdue (author of *The I Want to EggScape Book*) coined the verb "to EggScape (tm)" which means "to escape into another world with the help of decorated eggs" and "to create seascapes, landscapes and decorative scenes in, on, or around eggs." In her "Homage a Bob Ross" egg, a figurine of Bob, the TV painting instructor, stands on a craggy boulder painting a scene he sees before him which is, of course, the scene *we* see, peering into her egg. Mitzi points out the strategy of "infinite regress" which is a helpful concept here.

Along with other hints about proper foreground/background colors, and where to raise the horizon and how to properly stack or tessellate a mountain range to emphasize its essential—and necessary—imbalance, she says, "A good design principle to learn is 'Dead center is deadly.' Resist the 'sniper scope' approach, where you have the most important thing going on in the exact middle."

Right. The exact middle is not what this space is about.

It's 1861. Physician/writer Oliver Wendell Holmes is much taken with the stereoscope. "What a wonder it is, this snatch at the central life of a mighty city as if rushed by in all its multitudinous complexity of movement! There stands Car no. 33 of the Astor House and 27th Street–Fourth Avenue line. The old woman would miss an apple from that pile which you see glistening on her stand. The young man whose back is to us could swear to the pattern of her shawl...what a fearfully suggestive picture! It is a leaf torn from the book of God's recording angel...All is still in this picture of universal movement..."

Though the world has offered this space in so many different forms by now, each object or condition still presents itself as urgently as a hushed conversation, which, over the years, I have strained to hear, poised as I am, as this space requires, always at its edge.

Consider:

View-Masters, for instance: "Those modern day stereoscopes," reads the ad from 1946, "capture and contain famous American scenes, exotic faraway lands, exciting children's stories in the amazing depth of three dimensions—so real you'll feel you're actually part of the scene." Cowboy Stars. Firefighters in Action. Down on the Farm. Bullfight in Spain. Loch Lomand, Scotland.

"It's just like real," the ad continues. But it's the "likeness" that I like: the stunned and stunted back-lit drama, held still so I might not only see, but feel the measure of space—such small measure—between the dinosaur, cave, disaster, and me.

Slide viewers, where I can see pictures of my father's paintings without the walls of my parents' house and its furniture bantering in.

A snow globe's obedient, minute-long storm, churned in sealed silence. Where, into the eye of the storm, the body goes by way of sight, and stands below the swirling sky and settling drifts of square-snipped flakes, oh perfect and private dominion of stale water, plastic bridges, cluster of cabins, glittery, stoppered, and timeless.

It will, of course, take time to steer into, define, consider each object and condition listed and then to retire, refine or refuse it. Weigh its contributions. Recognize in it affinities, the family profile.

Jellyfish (though the live wires of nerves, those frilly oral arms distract a bit). Their bells, then, laced inside with white radial canals, and a pulsing, blooming red corona. Yes. And their buoyancy, transparency, fragility: the nimble, vulnerable gifts.

The space needn't be pleasant, since the way in which a thing holds still long enough to be seen isn't always. Nor is the yearning, the longing to see as when, through the rifle's scope, I closed the world down to one decision, and the thrill ran from finger, through arm and chest, to eye. How perfectly the finger served the eye!

Stoked the eye, assured the eye of its sovereignty in a blaze of smoke. And then a shattering fell from the sky, which broke, among other things, the space apart.

Or binoculars, through which I've watched my neighbor in his backyard shooting up. I could see the weave of dirty rope he used to cinch his arm, the tendons rigid in his neck as he bit down on the rope, pulled it tight, and angled the needle slowly in. And then, as he sat back in the lawn chair and waited, I could see, in the tondo the lenses made of sun-through-trees gold-leafing the leaves, the smoothing of his gaunt face, the slackening of every muscle as he slumped and nodded, slumped and nodded into peace.

I'm talking about a space that makes a place for thought, an air considerably pure in which objects—say, sugar bushes, sugar trees—grow precise in their stilled distance. Or perhaps things grow somehow distant in their precision, and hallowed as they are held. "A dreamlike exaltation of the faculties, that leaves the body behind," wrote Oliver Wendell Holmes, of his "fearfully suggestive" stereopticon.

Being separated from this space: the nightmare of artists: nothing holding still long enough to be seen. Or not being able to locate, use, train your medium to enter that space and fix on a thing. As Joseph Conrad wrote once in a letter to his friend and mentor Edward Garnett: "... I begin to fear that I have not enough imagination—not enough power to make anything out of the situation; that I cannot invent an illuminating episode that would set in a clear light the persons and feelings...." And this, in another letter, written during the same period: "Since I have sent you that part 1st... I have written one page. Just one page... the progressive episodes of the story will not emerge from the chaos of my sensations. I feel nothing clearly. And I am frightened when I remember that I have to drag it all out of myself." But it's not really a seizing of the imagination he is after I think; it's more a companionable pause, a palliative arm-in-arm stroll. One hopes not only for transportation but accompaniment. Sad moment, when my friend said, "I'm not painting now, but it's ok (he is brave: it wasn't), I'm painting in my head."

In the head? No. That won't do. I mean to be literal here. I mean the actual space between mind and work and how that slows, how that constitutes when one is at work, is working in the space. And I mean, too, the space art clears for us all—that place of density, interiority. I do not intend to be cozy. I do not intend to be abstract. I mean the actual space. *I like*, as Emerson said, *the silent church before the service begins better than any preaching. How far off, how cool, how chaste the persons look, begirt each one with a precinct or sanctuary.*

It needn't be pleasant, the space. And it is not necessarily beautiful. Connoisseur, you know it when you see it: not a watering system, timing, dispensing hourly, but a horse's scummy water trough. Not a neat scar, but a boil, inflamed.

Once I saw this: a man enters a tiny, dark room. He drops from his packet of coins, quarters, one by one, into a box on the wall. A metal shade rattles up and through the one-way mirror he sees, in a room beyond touching, three or four live! nude! women, contorting over easy chairs, rolling up pantyhose, unhooking each other, provocative, bored. Discussion, through the crackly intercom, costs more. He chooses only to watch. And that which is *watched* does not constitute the space. There are criteria to be filled...

As, too, in Faberge Eggs: commemorative (for coronations, marriages, and births). For historical occasions (the anniversary of the defeat of Napoleon; the Tercentenary of Romanov rule). With surprises inside: a miniature crown of jewels, basket of blooming diamond flowers, hen of solid gold. And the automata: a cuckoo clock; a walking elephant; and in the Trans-Siberian Railway Egg, a seven-car train with diamond headlights, ruby taillights, all set in motion with a tiny golden key. I cannot forget the Imperial Caucasus Egg, honoring the Romanov's mountain retreat, and decorated in the style of Louis the XV, with swags and garlands of gold and diamonds, and four tiny doors around the perimeter, pearl-rimmed, diamond-crusted, laurel-wreathed, each bearing a jeweled number of the date 1893 and opening onto a different painting of the retreat. Grand Duke George Alexandrovitch, Czar Nicholas's younger brother, was made to spend most of his time there in hopes the clear air and high altitude would ease his tuberculosis. A hidden memorial portrait of the Grand Duke can be seen inside by holding the egg up to the light and looking through the diamonds at either end.

It is colossally extravagant, of course, yet intimate, the way the sadness at the heart of any family is jeweled over. The way the secret emptiness at the heart of any album is held between its covers.

The earth, in Hieronymus Bosch's *Garden of Earthly Delights*, when the panels are closed, can be seen floating like a disk in a vitreous bell-jar: *that* space: yes. And too, when the panels are open, hell: all the gaping mouths choking on coins; all the blue-faced, human-stuffed gourds; anus-prisons with captives inside; hollowed geese rowed by monkeys; bodies cooking three-deep in cauldrons or pickled in spacious, rough-looking barrels; owls on eyeballs pecking them blind; cavernous pods spewing venom reserves; and yes, eggshell boats on flaming water; eggshell garths, spiky and airless; empty eggs with human faces and jawbone runners; eggs in which devils and bones with eyes strum tendony, dripping lyres. The most salient quality of Bosch's hell? Relentlessness contained. Emptiness filled with ferocious obsessions. Stages on which scenes play out—and play and play and play unending.

41

Let me crawl up toward the light for a moment with my hands and pockets full.

Not crystals, but geodes. In a geode's split, crystally center: that jagged, purpled cave where you could live with tiny crampons and ice picks, hunkered down, the light exploding all around.

A cauldron? No. Fresh eye of newt: certainly. Fresh eyes in handfuls, whole buckets of eyes? No. This is not a valu-space. This space cannot be supersized.

Frog spawn, those clear little globes of life, each with a pause and breath at its center, a comma thrashing, growing its thought.

Reliquaries, if the contents—even a shard of a shard, slightest splinter from Calvary or thread of raiment's hem or fingernail—is visible to the onlooker. Hesitation about authenticity (is that darkish crescent *painted* on the glass?)—fine. The glass can be dulled. The glass can be cracked and scratched and glaucous. Jewels can surround the lid: that's fine. Fine, too, all these centuries hence, that it must be viewed through another glass, the exhibition case. Distance isn't the problem. Nor is the rarefied, scented air of beholding.

Regarding light: fireflies—not in a jar, traditionally, but their bodies in air. Leaning close, looking fast makes the whole yard a jar. A flash-light: no. An oil-lamp: yes, its belly sloshing. A potbellied stove with iron plates removable with long iron handles: yes (and at the moment the plate is removed: the glow in there—but not the fire raging).

Chinese lanterns: those orange, papery pods gone lacy in fall, each with a dim, silver berry burning inside.

———

On Looking

A house lit from within at a distance—no. A house lit from within at a distance, in winter—yes.

A forest? No. But a shaft of sun through parted trees, the shaft itself cloudy, colloidal: yes. And come upon in a sudden clearing? Even better.

We shall move out of the forest, slowly.

And while we're at the forest's edge, in a meadow: split milk-weed pods, the silk mostly gone, just a bit still matted up inside. I like to think of an elf living there; an elf and not a fairy. Fairies flit around too much and leave that telltale, dusty sparkle. Elves can be spotted if you stay very still. (I don't actually use the word *elf*. But I know what I mean: a being aligned with a place and its story; a keeper of atmosphere, tonality, sensation, and the certainty he's there, unseen.)

Not a bird's egg, but eggs-in-a-nest. Seen from above at the Nature Center, irresistible the way they touch each other at one small point on the curvilinear: dirt-streaked and paint-spattered, tea-stained and rain-dotted, the eggs of the house wren, mockingbird, and crow.

I had a friend who, for Easter each year, got a bag of speckled birds' eggs in all sizes, from Germany. They tasted like what I'd always imagined a bird's egg, held in the mouth, would taste like: fresh, plain, milky-sweet. They lasted for days. After sucking them for a while, you had to put them away (on a plate, on the windowsill). They got smaller and smoother and disappeared—a kind of backward birth. These were nice, but then gone. So, no.

I knew someone who saw a nest he wanted—it was beautifully

constructed and hung darkly over a field's edge in the fall when the trees were bare—and he sawed down a tree limb to get it: absolutely not.

Picking up a sugar egg and putting the eye to it produced a mild dizziness, a sense of falling, of falling into it . . . just as there is falling involved in the presence of certain words, all palpable shade and tint and scene:

"Where were you?" "The *hall*." (no falling)

"Where were you?" The *foyer/corridor/vestibule*." (recondite, strange feel in the mouth, but, yes, falling)

"Where were you" Oh, *nowhere* (falling: kid's version, the kid discovered, listening in)

Eavesdropping (yes! Barest breath close against the door, shine of paint, fingernail idly along the grooved frame, the few clear words like little promises, tacit permission to be there).

Parlors (and parlours), if the drapes are drawn (not *shut* or *pulled* and God, not *closed*). And if it is between three and five in the afternoon and it is turn-of-the-century uncertain outside and at least one member of the household plays Chopin *(well*. And Liszt and Schubert too—why not? It is my parlor under construction). In there, the dark walnut furniture is beeswaxed to a pitch, higher up the scale of light than the neighbor's divan, she who's come to call and perches for an *interlude* (falling!) amidst armoires, ottomans, antimacassars, to listen to Chopin (oldest daughter, *Barcarole*), one son, "the little dauphin," scuttling through. The globelike lamps and the beaded lamps and, most important, stillest air. It must be unstirred, and one must stand gingerly at the threshold. Leaning into the room, over the velvet rope, permitted. Not to "get a better look" but to tilt out of the place where both feet are securely planted.

———

On Looking

Hands cupped around eyes: perfect; makes a parlor of anywhere.

It is tempting here to suggest "corner"—where, as a child, one is made to stand (where my son exiles himself, preemptively sometimes). But like the attic and the basement (no and no, except in recollection—then yes, powerfully, in recollection) a corner has to be entered with the body. And to enter that way dissolves the space as I know it.

Dutch doors, the top half swung open. (Leaning in.) Yes.

My father's boxes, dioramic, collaged, behind glass. In the early days, filled with simple wooden cones and spheres. Today, the objects and colors he uses conjure moments, compose atmospheres. There are deep blue night-backgrounds, empty piazzas, stamp-sized doors to open and close, black and white seas, silver birds, tiny bricks, crystal balls, red and green devils' faces. And when I gaze off, begin to consider what my father was thinking, and think I have before me the decisions he made about hanging this egg or gold-leafing that one, lining up the blue Buddhas next to all those Virgin Marys, when I think I know his intent, his desire, find a flare of intuition I think I recognize, I always look away. I turn back to the box itself, enter, and wander there. More than anything, I do not want to be outside, thinking.

I've always suspected the crystal ball was an aid, not a magical thing itself. I've always thought that looking into it and seeking that inversion, that high shine and upended swirl one could read the mind's wanderings, hold them, amid the argot of fate and the moment's demands, quietly enough to read.

Amber: the tiny faults and refractions, themselves translucent, like little rooms the sun has caught, walls it found as backdrop for— smallest gift—a fly locked in sap. A stanza is a little room from which

45

gifts emerge; also, in Italian: *a stopping place*. Like roadside altars, or shrines above busy intersections, in Rome or Florence—there behind glass and set into the building, where the eye travels up, rests from wandering and is rewarded for its pause, invited in.

A finger-sized doll I had whose home was a heart-shaped genie bottle, transparent and hinged at the bottom so you could pop her out to play. (I never popped her out.)

Dollhouses: yes, until the dolls move in and rummage around and start to talk. And wreck the penumbral, late Sunday afternoon of it all.

Not wasps' nests attached to the undersides of eaves or bare branches leaning low to the ground, chamber after chamber hunched together, silvery-crisp. Even in fall, when nests are often torn or pulled apart, so many chambers are tightly capped—and the others, too dark to see into.

The Madame Lulu box: a pill box I very much admired—and was given by Madame herself visiting from France. My attraction to the box was immediate, produced from the dark of her bag as she sat in our living room with her knees touching the coffee table. I cared not at all for the tiniest pills she tipped out, and only a little for the sweet dust I licked from the box after she transferred the pills to a second, plainer one. I saw only the blue, convex, enameled scene on top: a shepherdess resting in a bower (and this forever my definition of a bower). There was a castle in the misty background and a shepherd-boy so near, who—oh, it was terribly discreet but I saw the implications—bent over her. It was the depth of the scene I fell into, the arc they made, heads together, the tiny will-o'-the-wisp between them in the distance. The scene opened a room inside me into which I could peer, and about which, in college I wrote critically, as is still the fashion today when considering the pastoral. But I still love the box.

Perfume rings, their domes unlocked and there, the musky amber wax to dip into and spread along a wrist—*ambergris* it used to be, culled from the ears of whales. And poison rings, as they were called, holding bits of bone and snatches of hair from saints or martyrs, to gaze upon for luck and to ward off evil.

Music boxes? No. But trying to rig the ballerina to stay upright and so keep dancing when the box is closed and the space goes dark and musicless. *How* to keep her spring unbent, her tilted pirouette ongoing? To try with fishing line and copper wire. Peeking in, the box half-shut. Being *sure* there was a way, the afternoon's endeavor. (Slight fever, gray day, persistence.) Yes.

Deep in its peering, its leaning and looking, where is the body? Where (use the View-Master!) is the dinosaur, Rockette, icy waterfall? Where, oh where is Amelia Earhardt? I did so love her, and when I was ten, read all about her—crinkly eyes, faint splash of freckles, the soft, kid, aviator's helmet (so *that* was *kid!*). Yes. That moment when a word incarnates, finds its skin: yes.

A clear rattle filled with little multicolored beads: an hourglass-in-training. And a sand-filled, grown-up one, too.

On the boardwalk this summer I found the space in souvenir key chains; inside of each is a tiny photoed boardwalk that brightens when you hold it to the light, peer through the squared-off pyramid and follow the scene to its tiny, pinpoint perspective's end. And there you stand, eye to the hole, face to the light, looking at the place you're in, without you.

———

"The mystery of things, little sensations of time, great void of eternity! All infinity can be contained in this stove corner between the fireplace and the oak chest. . . . Where are they now I ask you! All those marvelous, spidery delights of yours, those profound meditations on poor, little dead things . . ." asks Oscar de Milosz.

Where?

A sugar egg is their temporary home.

Open air version: on the hill overlooking the Circus Maximus in Rome, the chariots gone; the racket of horses colliding, gone; the pile-up leaving a way for the lesser horse and that victory-by-default, all gone. Time doing its tricks, so the deep quiet enfolds. Even as the traffic rushes by behind you.

A camera: last century's, the head and back draped, one eye to the glass, for the long, dark passage toward oceanliner, great fire, beloved's face.

Sea Monkeys in a jar. Ordered from the back of an Archie comic. Aquiline, shirred: there he is. I'm sure that's the one, with his little gold crown, fuzzily perched: King Sea Monkey. And floating around, waiting to attend his Highness—all the Monkeys of his court. So that he might best survey his royal waters, rule his tepid kingdom from on high, I shall lift him onto my finger into the air. (Of course I don't. But I want to.)

Under a thirty-year-old microscope, the thirty-year-old slides showing the liver cells of a frog, their still-shapely coronas and gray, hazy stars. The heart of frog and bottlebrush spore, featherfowl point and butterfly scale. No longer "prettily a-moving" as Anton van Leewenhoek said of his animalcules, but held, stilled, still available— if a little yellowed, a little dry.

On Looking

The tiny person folded knees-to-chest contained in the head of a sperm, the homunculus in his watery world: yes. Even if a conjecture, and sketched from only that.

Leewenhoek destroying his specially ground lenses before his death, that hoarding: no.

The enormous prize bull at the Ohio State Fair, whose testicles stunned even the solemn farmers into low, whistling analogy, *cantaloupes, watermelons* (no kidding), as they stepped back. Stepping back: yes, lengthening the scene, so awe has a little room to breathe. That courtesy.

Not the real-but-stuffed bear in the dining room of the Pennsylvania brewhaus, but en route, the bear nailed to the barn wall, splayed like a star. The body aloft and flying, and the barn, a terrible, red wind behind it. And everything framed and reduced by the car window as we slowed down to get a better look.

What is gazing into a sugar egg? A way of being sealed away, destiny-less, in a sanctuary with no purpose at all, save being led. A way of being a child reading under a sheet with a flashlight. Half-moon shadows on the page. Finger eclipses over the words. And in the web between thumb and forefinger, the reddened streams of veins. The very river you're reading about, the mighty Mississippi right there. Right there in your hand, near the warm, pliable rim of shore.

Ships in bottles.

Lighthouses? No, because they have a job. But a lighthouse in a bottle: yes.

49

———

If, as Thoreau wrote, "A lake...is the earth's eye, looking into which the beholder measures the depth of his own nature," then consider, too, the ice of a lake into which things are frozen. Lake Erie ice, the sky griping on, unmelodious, moody, and someone's there now, at the end of the pier, in the very spot where I once was, looking over to Canada. If I were to go on about the cold that winter in Cleveland, my long flu, the solid grays scouring the sky, reminiscence would choke out the space I'm considering: there in the ice, stuff pinned with clear darts of air, and below that, the movement of water still visible.

Small pond in summer: leaning over the edge of a rowboat and seeing down through clear water. At the pool, with goggles: the rough bottom and a few pennies. In the ocean, tucking under the claw of a wave. I don't remember learning that trick, just one day being safely below and the force rolling over, grazing my back. The wild, colloidal spin just above and how quiet it was, and unlikely, that calm.

A cricket in a cage: the delicacy, lightness, quickness of the captured thing. The impermanence of those attributes, and of those bars. But while the cricket's in it, there's the ridge-and-file system of its wings, and you can see its song.

A blowfish, inflated, shellacked and spiky—and hollow as a mason jar.

Coral, held in the hand. The starry spaces bodies left, shallow but enterable.

The displays at the Museum of Natural History in New York. Not only because of the glass between us, but for the intercessory care taken—so that the distant mountain's painted shadow and the hunter-gatherer's shadow from the overhead lights do not overlap, there on the plains of Central Africa, where the "family preparing a meal" might, at any moment invite you in.

And while I'm in New York: window displays: their stillness amid the crowds, even if the little fisher-boy's rod dips in and out of a plastic revolving lake-surface, and even if the off-site fan is set to lift and float and settle the silk across the mannequin's ever-hardened nipples. Even though I sometimes am made to want what I see. Standing there, in the crowd, all the traffic noise eddying behind me—I cup my hands to the sides of my eyes, and though people cough (usually makes for a "no"—see "planetarium" below) and yell and jostle, and jumble their bags and exhort, they are, of course, supposed to be doing that. They're a *crowd*. And I, while standing and looking, am apart.

Not the planetarium—someone always coughs, disturbing the universe. Not the theater, not the movies: too many others admitted, your knee touching another's knee at one small point on the curvilinear, the whole of your musculature now distracting.

Alone with the visiting comet. Telescopes, yes.

Pressing a knuckle into a closed eye for the bursts, as I did when I was a child before sleep, so all kinds of time would collapse.

The way a busy street clears for a moment of its traffic, fills with the hum of emptiness, which throbs, which arrives like the moment a banner ends in its open-most unfurling. How long can it possibly last, that squall of silence, filling and surging, as loud as anything that's been calling and calling, unheard, all this time.

———

51

Lia Purpura

Bubbles. Only, briefly.

An apartment peephole, if you can tiptoe up, breathe very quietly, and do not intend to open the door.

Oven windows. Not-opening to peek.

Two of my friends got sugar eggs every year: Yvonne, whose family in Germany sent one at Easter, and Ilene, who was given a new egg at Passover. Ilene kept each egg (from Itgen's Coffee Shop in Valley Stream, NY) in its cellophane wrapping on a shelf. One was the size of a football; others were small, like walnuts or lemons or grapes. I loved to take them down and look at them when I visited, which was often. I was happy when, over time, the wrappings dried and fell off and I could hold the eggs' rough crystal curves in one hand and darken or brighten the scene with the other. Sometimes I came away with flecks of sugar on my hand. My sister and I never got sugar eggs.

Not getting: absolutely.

The Pin

Nothing can trouble the dominance of
the true image. Whether from graves or from rooms,
let him praise finger-ring, bracelet and jug.
—Rainer Maria Rilke

...a chair
beautiful and useless
like a cathedral in the universe...
—Zbignew Herbert

What the pin wants, sharp now and sprung, bright ache in the last green grass before winter, is its tension restored, hand in its pocket, head in its helmet again.

I'm leaving it there so I might come upon it, so what I call *today* might assemble —morning's low slant around the pin's open arc, late afternoon's autumn light darkening already as I walk home.

I do not touch it, do not fix it, and always, by the time I come upon it resting on the corner lawn of the sociologist's house, I've worked up to a good pace, full of intention. And there's the pin, a prize, a treasure, bright enough for a child to grab, but I do not close it. I want it to be as an equivalent, to match my surprise with its ragged grin, to surprise like desire come upon. The pin is the very picture of something undone—or an elsewhere falling apart from its lack. If I can call the pin *image, memento, moment suspended,* then the whole northeastern Ohio sky draws close, bends down here in Baltimore, and here come the cornfields along East College where, as a student, I'd ride my bike miles from town, south on Professor, turn east and be gone.

I'd ride for an hour, two hours and still not exhaust whatever it was I was trying to run out of myself. Along Hamilton Street, laundry hung on gray lines, even in the cold, in late October: boxy school jumpers, work pants in all sizes, the slate greens, the straight lines solemn and stiff, as I flew by. I'd slow down to pass the old Beulah Farm orphanage, its bare dirt yard and one-room school-house, and sometimes the orphans themselves playing behind the splintering fence. Mostly, there were fields and fields of corn, which in the spring made the back roads into intimate hallways striped with light where the stalks parted like doors creaking open.

Once in the fall, a friend and I biked far, past fields of harvested corn. We rode not talking much, comfortably silenced by the wind in our faces, one pulling ahead for a stretch, then the other, until cresting a hill, we saw a white farmhouse rise up. Yellow police tape crisscrossed the porch. Below the *Do Not Enter* sign nailed to the door, we tried the knob and it opened. I crossed over with my friend, who in the shaded living room, amid the scattered stuff of disaster I surely kissed. Or, after poking around for a while, it was he who brought something to show me, a stained, crumpled shirt, a week-old newspaper, and, bent together over the object, we breathed our few words near each other's faces, necks, closer still, until the decision to touch and be touched dissolved. It was something any of us would have done—used the props of the moment to frame, to give shape to our desire. Then, among pots on the stove with their lids askew, piles of mail, work coats and muddy boots by the door, the moment grew suddenly large. The weight of the unknown event, the lives we moved so easily among displaced us, and we left, quickly uncomfortable.

But while we stayed, we stayed because we were protected by a curiosity so certain of its task, that things—boots, mail, pots, our bodies—offered themselves, first tentatively and then with urgency, as if for us alone, solicitous as all objects of adoration, as all objects in stories lure us, irresistible and catalytic.

I felt certain nothing could happen to me in that house, or to him, even as we walked through the wreckage, because I could *see* us there. Even as we touched a few derelict things, isolated, stubbornly beautiful glass things—faceted doorknob, etched wedding goblet— even as he held up an old newspaper anxiously between thumb and forefinger, we were like characters caught in the instant of being created. Thus constituted, I watched myself leave the farmhouse even as I left the farmhouse, saw myself riding, even as the wind lifted my hair, downhill now and coasting fast, the fields on either side cut to stubble, the late afternoon clouds jagged and heavy as purple cliffs.

My bicycle was a blue three-speed clunker. I loved it inordinately. Riding to class, or home late after the library closed and town was shut tight, I'd practice feeling both its presence and absence. I would say, contriving nostalgia, "I loved swinging the bike under me and taking off" even as I swung the bike under me and took off. I'd fly, and see the moment of flight in my head. I lived preemptively with loss, memorializing instances. Even the names of nearby towns, whispered under my breath at odd times during the day, for the sound, for the shape alone, names redolent of small bars and lake-side ease and postindustrial collapse, were both present and simultaneously ancient, unreachable: Canton, Elyria, Lorain, Medina. Even as I walked and sat, ate and drank in those towns, I was a feature of their passing. Even then, another's body was both landmark and landscape, steep climb and descent, breath exchanged, passing current, wave, pulse, there, going and gone. And, too, my own body—mine and not mine, offered, recollected, offered again, until I could see its shape as my own, unequivocally.

Lia Purpura

I anticipate this pin, its sprung tension, and my own, as I step over. I am, every morning and every afternoon, with each going-out and coming-back, startled by its shine, by the light so surely illuminating its sharp tip, its faint rust, the disquieting thoughts that come. A terrible tenderness comes: the dry scratch of the failing Viceroy on my wrist, on my son's wrist, slow now, dusty and fraying midautumn; my neighbor, who practices writing her name because she is forgetting how the sounds go, what the letters mean. And from further away: at Point Lookout, on Long Island's south shore, the pale pink of a clam, its stomach in shreds, its inner shell a purple iridescence pooling water; the periwinkle, washed up at high tide, its milky scrim of muscle and row of blue jeweled eyes, drying.

And from further off still, this comes: the cloudy hexagonal window I peeked through on a class trip, and then unscrewed for myself to reach into the cow's first stomach, *the rumen*, I repeated. We were on a science outing and were meant to put our hands in and explore. We were given cheap, plastic gloves with long, scratchy seams that ran from shoulder to fingertips. "Won't this hurt?" I remember thinking.

The pin continues as a sliver of glass or jagged piece of shell on the beach continues. The sky here, now, is as low and vast as some other sky, elsewhere and past, and I step over: I, whose hand in a plastic glove swept through a cow's stomach. I, who was told the window in the cow's side, the *cannula*, still-awful word, didn't hurt at all. Imagine the child pairing the word "window" with "stomach", squaring the phrase "won't hurt at all" with "the cow's side is open for us all to touch." Imagine the child on a high, wobbly stool, sweating, itchy—it was early June—watching, beginning to narrate her own hesitation:

She pulled out a handful of cud and it was sweet-smelling. She was not the least bit afraid to press her face against the warm hide, to plunge her arm down and feel the stringy, matted stuff.

It wasn't fear, but the adults' insistence that skewed the scene.

"The cow never even notices the hands inside her stomach," and "go on, go ahead" they urged.

And though I did go ahead (I was a brave child), I could not make the moment grow, and I knew this resistance to be right. I could not make the cow a thing. That story would not unfold.

I keep in front of me always, on a sill or shelf, in every place I've ever lived since college, the jaw of a calf I found in a field. It was January in the Badlands of South Dakota. The cold was shattering; it left one literally breathless and coughing. One night the Sioux rancher I was staying with for the term got a call that part of his herd wandered out of the barn and their faces were iced to the ground. In the blackness, he and his sons dressed and went out with blow torches to free them and bring them back in. I did not live for long on the Reservation; I was only working there for a while. But I have the jawbone with its planes and curves, and I can see, anytime I look up, the darkened patches, the curtains of teeth, their folds and pleats, the porous, roughened bone with grays and creams, and where the light finds a translucent patch, a delicate near-pink.

I keep it because, as forms go, it's shapely, beautiful. I might say, more accurately, it speaks to me. There's a crescent-shaped hole where a cord once went through, a few teeth are broken and the joints only partial, but it gathers around it the idea of what flesh used to be. And in that way becomes substantial, softens, contours, draws around it the possibility of what once was, the story of another life.

If the thing is a form desire takes, I like to be reminded of that, going out, coming back, stepping over the pin, morning, afternoon, the pin dangerously open and tense and snagging the available light.

Red: An Invocation

I remember the fox in the light I drove forth. It was just before dawn. The headlights lit the fox's eyes, who did not blink but passed the light back, so it shone between us. Two beams of dust in colloidal silence spread and touched the dark brush by the side of the alley. The fox was ember-colored, fresh-snapped, and already cooling.

*

Later that morning, I remember seeing nothing at first but a puff of crisp leaves, a burned smear in a tree. Then I stopped below the hawk. On the scythe-curve of its breast, I remember the color as blood-dried-in-air, as the rough, indeterminate edge of a notion, just forming. I remember thinking "it looms over us," then saying aloud "looming over" and then, to better myself, to sharpen my sight, when it flew I said "the air of the loom."

I was walking my son to nursery school when I saw how the notion forming was poised, with hawklike curves, with foxlike silence.

Lia Purpura

With that red.

Red, come toward me. Stay, as I walk with him. Shorten the distance from this teeming place to that, as we cross, as we ford with one step, another, and another, ford as a pioneer girl did—the year is 1846, vast with rivers and mountains—and who, casting back for the story's beginning, mid-summer before the terrible snows, before Donner Pass was so named, wrote: "let me say that we suffered vastly more fear... before starting than we did on the plains."

*

I looked along the hawk's burnished body, its smooth burnished weight. But "burnished?" No.

And "red" for the body of the fox isn't right, though when you look, as you might for long minutes if you've never seen a fox before, not like this, so still and so close, you'd see, not red exactly, but how the color is a form, recognizable: a particular concentration inhering, a body's signature reflex and decision. The barest gesture we know a thing by, and by which, in a breath, it is gone.

*

"As she forded the schoolyard, the loom of warm air shuttled fast above, and she took her son's hand..." I wrote of myself in my head as we walked, though I did not point the hawk out to him.

*

The moon was still just a sliver, and the light I drove forth showed the fox's front leg held aloft, strictly still: it could not know if this was the light of kindness or a killing spot, and so with one leap, all deftness and economy, the fox slipped into the underbrush, wholly

60

out of sight. As it disappeared, the tail of the fox was a wisp, a streaked, feathery plume.

As the hawk lifted up, its brushfire tail was barely a rustle. That is, that morning, the hawk with the breast of a useful blade, with its breath and intention and hunger contained, took off from the highest, steady branch. Its underwing red, its shoulders red-dipped.

By *red* I mean the last thing I could see as the hawk disappeared.

As the fox slipped away.

And yes, I led my child into that day.

The Smallest Woman
in the World

...said the red letters on the painted measuring stick at the Maryland State Fair. It was a hot, darkening day, the sky holding off rain. Between the play-till-you-win fishing game and made-to-look-old carousel, there was her booth. The Smallest Woman in the World.

Do you want to see her, I asked Joseph and his friend, Denis. Yes, they said. It was only fifty cents. Ania, who just told us that she was afraid of big characters in costumes and so would never go to Disney World, figured she was not going to like a very small person either, and stayed out. The man at the entrance returned her fifty cents, in dimes.

Joseph and Denis went into the tent and peeked behind a cubicle, gray and fabric-covered like in an office. I saw them waving. Waving *back*, since at seven, they wouldn't have thought to do so on their own.

Yes, a heart can sink. A heart can drop as fast as a white rock in a clear river, a dry leaf in white water. A heart can sink far from sight, the misstep above chipping the rock, the pieces hitting each outcrop down the steep cliff: there was a folded blue wheelchair in the corner. There was a cheap wheelchair I was hoping the boys wouldn't notice.

Because then she'd be small-because-hurt. Small-due-to-problems. Not little-pal small. Not hold-her-in-your-pocket-magically-small, like a coin or a frog. Not small as a secret, or the very idea of a dog waiting all day outside the school fence—just for you.

Hoping they didn't see *what?* The way the chair leaned into the makeshift corner? Its blue, tarplike back? Its own terrible smallness? How its careless placement broke the illusion of small-for-small's sake?

I stayed out of the tent. I wasn't going to leave Ania alone, with her fear of large characters transforming. I could not let her stand there while I went with the boys, who of course, also needed to hold a hand while looking.

Looking at what?

The Smallest Woman in the World.

Now, weeks later, Joseph still can't sleep and comes calling: *I'm thinking of the smallest woman in the world. Why?* And: *When will I stop thinking of her?*

When I was eighteen, and in college, I began to think a lot about being seen. I remember not wanting to be seen "as an object." And that we insisted on being called "women." But just a few weeks ago, walking past some old, drunk guys on the stoop of a neighborhood bar, I reversed my position. I let them look. I allowed them the sight of me. I mean I did not scowl and did not turn sharply away. At eighteen, I'd have been edgy and hard; I'd have walked past with my shoulders angled to cover my body. But I walked by them thinking, "If this is all you have, if all you can do is look, then here, *look.* Take it all in." It was easy to do, though not enjoyable. If it was some sort of sacrifice, it was not hard—first profile, then a full frontal view. What do you want to see—some ass passing by? The swing in my walk? And you, some breast? I was on the way to meet a friend and had been singing a John Pryne song I like these days: "Somebody said they saw me, swinging the world by the tail, bouncing over a white cloud, killing the blues."

You're seeing me killing the blues, I thought—you're seeing that, right?—the white cloud, the world by the tail? Because I'm in deep, and somehow that's clear to you three, who have been drinking, it must be, for hours already, though it's still early morning. I'm killing the particular blues I've got by laughing a little at your stupid, raw comments, by turning toward and not away, and the amber liquid is tilting a line, like—so clearly it comes back—the cross section of a glacial lake up against its perpetual glass in the Museum of Natural History back in New York. What you're holding in your hands, in that bag, is terrain. What I am is—terrain. Map me, then, Sailor. Lay me out. Say you're just passing through and want to see a sweet thing before you leave port.

But she wasn't passing through. The boys were. They walked up to the cubicle and waited and waved. And stood for a moment and waved again. And then turned to go—as she must have turned from them, and back to something at hand, at rest in her lap. *Enough*, her eyes must have indicated. *That's all you get.*

I did not see what my son saw. He went out without me and now he's lost there, in the scene, with her, though she was *nice*, he assures me. She had a plastic jack-o'-lantern of candy she was eating from. A *jack-o'-lantern*, I asked? Yes, he said, with her hand digging in it. It was August. And that gesture, that image, will displace him for weeks: the jack-o'-lantern in summer. The candy unoffered. Her own private stash. And was there a book, tableside, she was reading? A tiny TV? My own questions keep coming. Does that man make her sit there, my son asks and asks. Is he mean? Is she happy? Does she want to be there? Mom, why am I sad? Is it because I looked at her like she was a sculpture? Why is he advertising her?

65

Lia Purpura

———

The other day, in the early September sun, I walked for a block or so to try this out: hands behind my head and elbows out, to take up a lot of room, like the guy who had just passed me. He was walking down a wide, shady street, at home in the ease of his body's expanse. And yes, walking that way, I take up a lot of room, as he did, but there's this: when my hands are behind my head, my breasts lift up. Am I freer because I take up more space, or less free because now I'm even more seen? Do I provoke more attention, erode my own space, invite, by the provocation I cannot help being, another's gaze into the scene?

I just want to be that guy, arms up in the cool air, my shoulders and neck stretching, lungs open, ribs rising.

I want to lift my shirt and scratch my stomach as a friend of mine does wherever he likes. "I do that?" he asks. Yes, you do, I point out—in the kitchen, in the store. On a walk. Wherever you like.

When will I stop thinking of her? my son asks and asks.

I have a friend who goes to strip joints. (And who, by the way, has written surprise compassion into those scenes, real compassion, the kind that shows he knows the below-deck of all the whirling hers in the dark surround: working mother, or artist, activist, would-be accountant. How formal and graceful his words become when touching, yes, touching, that other.) I have another friend who subscribes to *Playboy*. (Who thinks it's more the anticipation—article, article, article: photo!—than the photos themselves that . . . do it for him.) What do I think about that, he asks. What do I think of his subscription. I tell him: why not? As in: go ahead. Live it up. I say *why not?*—because I, too, like to look. At everything. To see myself. To see myself being seen. Though *Playboy* certainly used to bother me. A lot, when I was eighteen. My son, reading his cousin's 1970 collector's edition one morning this summer when we were visiting, woke me saying "This is disgusting! Why are their clothes off?" At five a.m., this was all I could muster: I said it isn't disgusting, that the body is beautiful and it's natural to be naked, but the magazine isn't for kids. Not at all, hand it over.

My son still thinks, by way of the perspective in photos or drawings in magazines that some people are really *very* small—say, two inches high, and you can hold them in your hand. Just pluck them out of the photo and pocket them. He wants to know where they live. A boy in Sudan on a tiny barren hill. Can I take him? he asks. *Home*, he means, and *can I hold him here safely?*

There's a scene I remember from college, an image so sharp and clear and impressive I remember thinking, *you'll retain this*. It was my last year and I was standing outside the militant vegetarian co-op with a friend, talking. And I stopped, just stopped midsentence, and she looked in the direction I was looking. "He's *cute*," she said. But that wasn't it at all. I was aware of his beauty, and of my easy desire, but more powerful still, I wanted to *be* him. I wanted the angular frame and slim hips, low belt and button-flys resting just so. I wanted the T-shirt's sharp fall from his shoulders to fall from my shoulders. For a long moment he didn't even have a face. I couldn't unravel the two desires: I wanted to look and to touch, yes. But more than that, really, I wanted to *be him*.

I look now, at forty, more like him than ever. I've pared down. I wear my pants low, with a belt and I tuck in my T-shirts, simple white T-shirts or green or black ones. And though I've lost the wide hips of a new mother and the full breasts for feeding, the lines of me are still rounded. Is this a body a man would want to inhabit? Would a man want to be—I mean walk, sleep, move—in this frame?

When I started to read the *Little House on the Prairie* books to my son, I was prepared. While I loved the characters, and identified with them fully—the sisters whose hands were cut from twisting straw into makeshift logs for the fire, their bare faces browned by hot, summer sun, their calico dresses, the rough crunch of batting and ticking at night as they slept—I was prepared for him not to like the books. I was ready for him to say "this is for girls." But he didn't. Not once. I believe he felt that slightest membrane between bodies, that he saw how easily one form can inhabit another. There, on the prairie, in the dug-out, the lean-to, he tasted their water, cool from a dipper. He slapped down the bread and basted by lamplight. He sang with the family. He blew out a candle. He slept with a quilt.

He wanted to be one of them.

As he very much did not want to be small, and displayed at a fair in the heat of August.

The Space Between

Now, more than hitherto, there occurs shocks, surges, crossings, falls and almost scrambles, creating thus a different space, a space scattered and unknown, space enclosing spaces, superimposed, inserted, polyphonic perspectives.

—Henri Michaux

Where is the fear this afternoon? Where did it go and why can't I locate it now?

A goldfinch flies up while leaves, gold and russety, sift and fall. A flight up, a flight down, the very air marked, so both rising and falling are held in a furor of sunstruck ongoingness.

I am outside this bright afternoon.

And even as I am built anew by fear these days, here, in Baltimore, I am also, right now, assembled by the brisk feel of New England, and fall, and my childhood there. That peace. Those biting blue skies. The elements mingle, brick by brick (though the sensation is softer and welling) and add up to this moment, a seep and twining that constitute *now*. Of course, this moment has little to do with simple construction, simple addition. But it's hard not to think in these terms.

I'll try again.

Events crosshatch: the air this afternoon is cleanly scented, still unstark, and in it, among sheering leaves, among goldfinches lifting and scalloping air, a sniper—in a patch of woods, gas station, mall parking lot—is hiding, aiming and shooting.

And here, too, is the heavy sweater I'm wearing, thin at the elbows, the bruisy ferment of old apples, leaf dust, clouds stacked high in the west, *peace*.

Other things, too, are stacking up today: campaigns for Maryland's governor, though few of us now seem to notice, so frightened are we to pump gas, to let the children walk to school. *Candidates must wrest control of voter attention*, the paper says. "Rest" I say to my son, who learned from other kindergartners there's a bad person out there shooting, my son who's going to take it easy this afternoon, play Crazy 8's, maybe a little chess, inside.

Inside such perfect weather, an investigation is mounting. State Mounties are out on their horses, horses such as the angry men mounted this evening as they rode out of De Smet, Dakota Territories, to a riot at Stebbins camp, deep in Montana, 1878, I read to my son as he went uneasily to bed. As the Ingalls family rested uneasily *By the Shores of Silver Lake*, in the perpetual *now* that is book time. The children tucked in, the lake serene, the riot ongoing in moonlight, *on a night just like this*, I point out the window and up, to where "the great round moon hung in the sky and its radiance poured over a silvery world. Far, far away in every direction stretched motionless flatness, softly shining as if it were made of soft light." The moon outside Joseph's window. The very moon that swallowed both that writer's fear, and mine.

See how the moments go layering up?

These days, late afternoons in our small living room, a form unfurls and spreads its weave—music building and cloaking, uncloaking and reaching. The fugue my husband is working on makes available to light, and with a light of its own brings forth a moment: amber with its captured specks, bubbles of breath and veering planes. And across the country, now, right now, in that other Washington, where it's a

still-bright two in the afternoon, there's a search on for bullets a
suspect once fired into a stand of trees. In a quiet neighborhood, ATF
agents saw down stumps and haul them away in trucks as evidence.

Consider their find: cross-sectioned rings interrupted by bullets,
all the loops of years pierced.

The loops of years pierced and containing the point.

This time of year, when the sky darkens early and clouds stack up
in thick, western swells, I see therein a mountain range I once knew.
(The sniper, we will come to learn, had a mount for his gun in the
trunk of his car: the trunk of his car a small terrain of roughened
upholstery, the gun at rest there, those beveled edges along the
muzzle, the boredom of waiting, his fingernails scraping up curls of
grime, flicking them off. Sun in a beam through the punched-out
lock reaching a summit, casting its curves.)

Let me come back, though, to the matter at hand.

When the sky darkens and clouds rise like a near mountain
range, my neighborhood plunges into a valley, makes of itself one of
the small, snug towns I loved as a child in New England. I'd like you
to believe, as I wanted to believe, that I actually "lived as a child in
New England," for I felt such familiarity when visiting, as if I'd found
a home I hadn't known I'd lost—in Great Barrington, East
Hardwick, at our friends' small farm in Clarkesville, New
Hampshire, way up near the Canadian border.

What it *is*—is what *else* it is. Not just that this afternoon's thick,
boulder-clouds resemble the mountains I loved as a child, but that
the one scene collapses in on the other, time reworks and folds
together. And I live in both places.

What it is—is what else it is. For this reason I am often startled
by the simplest gestures of things: a leaf scratching along sideways
moves as a crab does, so much so that the animal's likeness comes
powerfully in, and the shock of seeing a crab on the sidewalk trumps

reason. And though I tell myself "it's fall; *leaves* dry, scratch and blow, not *crabs*," I'm jittery walking down the street—not frightened exactly, I can't say afraid—but always the scene I'm in breaks open and floods. The stuff of an *elsewhere* comes in, as when, among the dried, speckled shells of crabs this summer, a snowball rolled ocean-ward before returning itself to a clump of sea-foam. The flap of an awning blows in wind—and it's a low-flying bird's wing. The dark underside of a mushroom's gills, grown tiered and up-curved after rain, makes a tiny Sydney Opera House. Right there, hillside of the reservoir. Australia, just a few blocks from home.

I mean to say, too, that it's not all jittery, these exchanges. I remember seeing, at my uncle's house, a cat's brain, preserved, and how the brain's topography slid into more: a crush of continents ribboning up, river-valleys gone to inclines, post-glacial, scoured and jarred. And how standing in front of the pen-and-ink drawings of neurons, those cells were stretching, wavering blooms, tributaries, sidewalk cracks.

Things pair up to go forth.

When I am clear enough to catch it, it's the motion of Bach's Prelude XIV, the sense of it-all-going-on-at-once, one voice seeding always the next swell, unending, the swell out-spinning, the strands of sound buoyant, a weave tightened and cinched like the lip of a purse until the last tilt, and the pucker of folds lets the gold go.

And my husband's sure fingers are cresting sound as they have moved over all that I am, and all I am overrun by.

I came across this a while ago: "In music the distance and the nearness of space, the limitless and the limited are all together in one gentle unity that is a comfort and a benefaction to the soul."

The space *a comfort*.

A *benefaction*:

And *what* in the soft air, the chalk-blue of the blue spruce, the sky orange and pink just the other morning as I took the garbage out— *what* ferried me past my fear? What brought me instead to my old summer job as a coffee vendor, lower Manhattan, awake before dawn on Avenue C, the junkies cooled off, the Bowery wide and dank and mine to share with the bakery trucks, the newspaper trucks, just a few of us going out, a few coming home. Here's the blue dawn air settling over the cart I readied at my corner in front of Trinity Church, at Wall Street and Broadway—here now, in October, at six a.m., and fifteen years later.

What is it that took this morning over, washed it with a morning past and by that breath, kept from it the fear—who next will be shot?—also going on, right now. Right here.

Above this scene? Beyond it?

Where?

What about this, from Emerson's journal: "The universe is a more amazing puzzle than ever, as you glance along this bewildering series of animated forms—the hazy butterflies, the carved shells, the birds, beasts, fishes, insects, snakes, the upheaving principle of life everywhere incipient, in the very rock aping organized forms. Not a form so grotesque, so savage, nor so beautiful but is an expression of some property inherent in man the observer, an occult relation between the very scorpions and man. I feel the centipede in me, cayman, carp, eagle and fox. I am moved by strange sympathies."

Strange, yes, this sympathy, clearing a space, preparing a ground for meetings to occur—but fragile, too. Terribly fragile. So why, *why*, I have been wondering, did my friend, standing at the shore one night this summer, watching the white breakers arc, curl and fall— why did she say, even as the chill spray hit our faces and we shivered in relief from the day's heat, *how* could she say "it's just like a movie"? And pull us from the evening damp, the woody, splintered boardwalk, sweet ache of leaning on the chest-high railing, rumble of the arcade fading, folding in and out of wind. Why break the hum and echo of the moment we were in? Why leave the moment just then forming, moment that would, some morning, some evening, return to her a quality of light or air or scent and displace the sadness she might be feeling?

I've never been able to conjure, in winter, summer's heat. I cannot, by will, regard the snow into a fringe of green. So while I believe the sniper will be caught, I cannot summon that peace, nor compose a time without this pulse of fear. I only know fear comes to me. And also peace.

On October 24th, hours before dawn, the sniper is caught, with an accomplice, sleeping at a rest-stop near Myersville, MD. It's been twenty-five days now since the rampage began. Eleven people are dead. And though the snipers are locked far from us now, a world away—three miles away, just downtown, in hyperbolized space (Supermax, the *sine qua non* of desolation)—*here* they still are, large in their absence, and circling. Fall, like an axis, collected them in, spooled all the fear up.

Fall also spun around itself translucing yellows and flaming red stems. Last flocks lifting whole into trees for a rest, leafing back the empty spots, and late afternoons, a neighbor's carrier pigeons let out for a spin, angling like a single wing, an arm crooked up to block the glare. Thick pumpkins. White mums. Fall gathered these in.

And fall gathered, too, on this afternoon, my husband working up Prelude XIV; my son and his friends dropping split, rotting walnuts, *thunk*, in tin pails; the blade of air sharpening as the temperature falls; box elder bugs swarming the shed's southern wall—and everything, everything else uncountable, unaccountably part of, that constitutes *now*. And all this I call *fall*, I call *late afternoon*, will come back, will come hauling its wedge of cold fear, its unbidden relief, oh who can know which, some long summer hour when lines of road tar loosen in heat, a boy sits idly peeling a stick, and wood wasps drill slow, perfect circles in eaves.

Coming to See

Windows: Now and Then

I'm sitting in front of a clean, paned window. It looks out on a field but, floor to ceiling, the scene is filled by honeysuckle, its sweetness and low buzz crowding in. Above, two oaks lean in from either side and touch. Through the chinks in the bush I can see the field lead, in scraps, to a far stand of pines.

Yesterday I wanted to cut back the green tangle, so close to the house and obscuring the field, but I am just a visitor here.

I'm sitting in front of a clean, paned window, facing the mess of yellow-white-green. Here is my chance to see how bright the partial can be, the particular *now*. Last year when I stayed in a house nearby, my window framed a different field. But the window was screened and blurred my gaze so I had to focus on the sprawl of big forms— silver silo, far white fence—to keep my sight from slipping into the gray crosshatch of wire. I blinked and blinked to adjust my gaze.

I remember I wished for a clear pane then. A small, simple view. The distance contained.

Lia Purpura

Parts and Wholes

The sun, angled low in the early morning, makes the window gauzy in streaks. Branch-shadows switch darkly across my face and slowly, from the wash of green, things step forth: the seedling ash as thin as a finger, but plush with leaves, notched and saw-toothed, as big as those on the full-sized tree; the milk-blue moths and the buttery ones. Two branches of honeysuckle stand straight up, lean into the place the bush will go next.

I missed the deer but saw in parts, through the bush, small bits of brown, a flicking of cream. A dipping of white as it stepped along. A brief drought pulling across the field as the deer moved into the woods beyond.

And now, because I missed the deer whole, I want to cut back the honeysuckle —*just enough to see* I think. *See through.*

To *more?*

To *beyond* and *not here?*

I am thinking that cutting can shift a thing—release a space, be a new pattern laid.

That clearing a space is like crafting a question.

First Cutting: Opening

I asked my host if the honeysuckle is ever pruned in front of this house. I thought it might be rude to ask, but he said *No, if you want you can. Here*—he went to his car—*I just bought these clippers yesterday.* He squeezed the red handles, demonstrating. *Do what you like.*

Dew weights the new growth and wets my hands.

And now there is thistle. Now a sight line. Already a goldfinch looping up. Already I am not satisfied, the field a bright glimpse and I want only more.

Had he said *No, we just let it all go,* I would have settled in with the

76

tangle, learning it, diagnosing its moment-to-moment gestures. I would have studied the overleafed patches by which the distance was parceled and cut. Come to leaf ribs and spines in motion, the sound of rain sifting. Would have gone in and down, where, in the thick, matter intercedes for matter and leads to still more—recombinant, shapely.

But I wanted distance to unscroll my sight, for the grasses' bright tips to draw my eye out, far, to that jittery open.

*

I have not yet said that all this is occurring while my friend back home is dying. And that her dying is a hand upon it, a breath upon it and a frame.

Into the Open

This morning, early, I cut back more so the honeysuckle would tip like a cup and the field pour forth rye, milkweed, and chicory. If I knew better the kind of work I was doing, this work with distance, proximity, and sight, I could give it a name—for example, *I'm painting*. And purple the trunks, make of the blue-through-far pines an odd spurt, a shot brightened, as if a spring were caught rising. Looking out, I could think *so this is a bower*, stand at the easel and feel the solidity of the room behind me. Feel the dark filling, like a theater, lending purpose to my gaze.

But I could go further: clear-cut the brush to the edge of the field. Topple the trees that arc into this scene.

Yank the white curtains at the window's edges.

Then where would I go?

Shave the panes down and when the glass loosens, push the glass out. Climb over the sill. Turn to the house.

Lia Purpura

Burn the house.

Now in the entirely open field. As my friend is.

Is made to be.

What do you do in an open field—if it one day *occurs*, is *come upon?* Sun and shade striping, the green lapping, tidal, the tide its own thinking. The laps and relapse, all the internal shifting. If there, in the field, is a threat circling, a fin in the green, in the too-green field. Swimming so fast. Relentlessly swimming.

Interruption

If I went out to the apple and cut the black branch that hangs in my view, I could see, past the tree, a white spray of phlox, the flowers like sun spots, sudden in the field. The hanging black branch is swinging, distracting: it's the slip of a pen, or a brush stroke misplaced. A flaw in the scene, too precisely *there*.

Field as Body

Where the glass warps, the far trees ripple with weird internal banners. I look through the glass refracting the field, making it fold and slip and blur. Out there is a bird drilling into rich hollows, breaking them down, taking the field, part by soft part, into its body.

Dissembling

The end of the day swells like a breaker, holds itself curled against the green field. Keeps itself brief above the grasses. Keeps itself sheer before it falls.

Now in the half-light above the field, the day is something vanished-but-present, or present-but-going. A crest then a wobble, hovering.

I remember the game *move-dusk-to-dawn:* at the end of the day how we reeled back our bodies, making-believe.

How we made, for long moments, the rising and sinking alike.

Second Cutting: Belief

I push myself up from the chair after sitting and reading, and because I have been lifting heavy things in the last few days, moving furniture in this small house, and pruning, I feel a mild, affirming ache. Then I hear it.

At first I think wind is swelling-receding, filling the trees so they'll lift and sigh flat. But then the exhalation keeps on, elongates, and looking up, it's rain, that long, rolling boil, boiling over. Crushed honeysuckle is scenting the air. In the field beyond, timothy jackknifes.

More distance clears.

I think I can make that happen again, so in the damp after-mist, I go out to work on the big dripping branch that interrupts the whole field. And once it is gone I can see further still. I relax my gaze. It feels like driving, the field stretching out. Like I am moving. Moving toward.

Mist and Force

By morning, a fine, light sifting comes down, a wetness that isn't exactly rain: a roiling mist like motes of dust; a prickling damp; pinpoints beading up the field.

As out-and-out rain the wetness fails.

For silent, inexorable growth it is perfect.

All night the damp gathers. By morning everything green is bent under its diligent weight.

Lia Purpura

Decline

The dark spot on the window was an ash leaf days ago. It curls like a lip. It draws the eye to it.

Beyond, in the field, two purple finches meet above the thinnest grasses. They dip and hover—too heavy to land, but wanting the seed—then fly off to sturdier brush to rest. But my eye returns: the spot softens and browns. It worsens each day. In it, the gathered refusals of sun. In it, a thumbprint of heat and bruised air.

Body as Tether

In the three weeks that I've been here, the phlox has seeded itself in the field.

I can hold my arm out and squint, and one of the new blooms is a fingernail away from the first. I can lie down in the field and, reaching in any direction, touch one. But then there's another and another beyond that.

Scattered and dotted, I cannot hold the flowers together in any bounded way. I cannot corral them, not with my arms flung wide, or my sight. They cluster and bend. They come up all over.

The field is a tide the flowers ride out—far past the body I am using as measure.

Song

I try to make the step-down call of the chickadee, but do it too insistently, over and over so it loses sense, the air going equally out and back, not slower in the opening, then quickening as the tight hinge retracts, but absolutely evenly, too even, the way one breathes and regulates breath for a doctor, to present the body's equanimity. There's a bird in a tree with a hinge in its throat, a door opening to let the sweet air pass from a high, thin place down a notch. There's phlox out there, opening between one black and another black, hanging branch of an apple tree—the very tree that holds the bird that bends the air so parenthetically around itself, and its song around anything listening.

Tally

A web across the honeysuckle shifts light like beads on an abacus. Back and forth, doing its sums, it golden subtractions.

Third Cutting: Rising

It's some kind of butterfly: orange and black but smaller than the Monarch, smaller, too, than the Viceroy, something crazier that dips and flies up, scallops the air, looks like a kite a child is coaxing. Across the field its path is all sharp peaks and perfect troughs. *Across the field* means the whole way is clear and uninterrupted.

I look into the distance. The disheveled air above the green is a field itself, a haze of new heat where insects bob, slipknot, and careen.

Now my eye finds the dark edge of the field with ease.

Even after all my work, the low brush and honeysuckle were still too close—too close to the house, too close to sight, and so my host came with big clippers and chopped the rest back.

And when he clamped the blades around the base of the bush and pulled the long wooden handles together, he made a little grunting sound. I heard it from inside the house, the intimacy of dismantling, and then a softer rustle as he pulled the branches free. His exhalation, that smallest breath came for the bush and marked its falling.

Then: a confetti of moths in a freshet of air, rising because the way was clear. Scraps of distance seaming up, all the flecks caught in rays, the motes aloft.

A dragonfly slowed midair, hovering like a coppery breath.

Then the oddest ache came: a body that small, and everything *works*—the up and the down inseparable, thoughtless; the motion-as-stasis; the most perfect eyesight; the two sets of wings, their colors like pangs of disbelief.

The way through the field is entirely clear. There is nothing between the far woods and me—just motes, moths, mouths, that coppery breath, the whole raucous force rising, breathing and turning.

Return

The wild turkey moves with her chicks across the field, dips her head down and raises it, eating and picking in no hurry at all. Then she settles into the tall grass. I have the whole field, the view thrown wide, the rolling and sifting, but the liveliest part is not for the eye. She stays and stays. I want her to come out again, and when she does, her head is a spot of reddened grain.

The Whole

With no dormer of green framing the sky, no honeysuckle scrimming the light, I expect the field now, the whole arrayed, expect the wide sweep in front of me—the curled fists of new ferns, the milkweeds' closed hooves among the tall grass. Thistles. Daisies. The clamorous reach of purple asters.

Further off, the turkey is a drop of sound, *oak, oak*, far back in its throat, *oak*, wetly and darkly, only the sound burrowing in, finding a spot in the sway of grasses. The grasses lapping like a body of water.

Darknesses

Everything in the field has a name, one the eye pulls from the wash of green to steady itself: *saw grass, timothy*. And where the field stops and the woods begin? *The abrupt edge,* bird watchers say, a sheltering darkness made wholly of green.

Reprieve

Earlier in my visit, she would have appeared in smudges through the tangled brush, a flash of red, her brown-flecked body a crumple of patterns. Now she steps, for long moments, into the open.

Nearby, the chicks are learning their way through the field. A cool, almost cold breeze blows, and they stop. And when they move off again, they're into the phlox.

I see the stalks crush underfoot.

I can see, too, the chicks following her. And when they scatter into the field, how they part the long grass like rivulets and are gone.

Imperceptibly, as a day deepens.

As my friend is going.

As the distance is going, piecemeal to the edge.

Lush edge where sight stops and the body goes in.

(in memory, Margot Bos Stambler)

Falling Houses:
mise-en-scene

I know someone who drops houses.

Small houses. Condemned ones. He buys them for nothing and uses cranes and helicopters to haul, then drop them from on high, then he drops the pieces until they reduce to sharp angles and wire and corrugation, and he photographs the drops.

For a while I just looked at the photos—the colors, the angles, the motion. The order of descending shapes. The evolutionary lopping of edges, the cracking of form.

Now I don't know what to think. But I think I'm supposed to be thinking. So here goes:

The subject doesn't seem to be the ominous destruction of the family.

The process isn't wasteful, since the houses are going to be demolished anyway.

I read that the artist doesn't like to talk about how he does it—that he "never intended the process to be a concern for the viewer."

He just takes the pictures and presents them, massive and simply framed. He is "happier when people react to the actual image."

But then, his catalog provides all these sneak peeks at the process...helicopters positioning houses for a drop; the cluttered work sites; rented trailers and folding tables loaded with lunch; plans unscrolled like blueprints; disembodied fingers pointing; the artist, central in white T-shirt and jeans, walkie-talkie clipped to his belt wearing his regulation hard hat.

So now I'm thinking about ruins, the conscious creation of ruins.

I'm thinking that to ruin a thing, one must behave like time and weather, assume the prerogative of the elements. Or the point of view of a child standing over a dirt world, finger outstretched, alert to his shadow darkening the hills. The foot-soldier ants. The rain rivulets coursing through towns, pebble roads, rosebud cars. Raise a hand up, bring a hand down. One must have a mind for roughshod turns of phrase to say *create a ruin*.

I suppose these might be models of houses hung against blue backing, plush velvet for texture and to absorb the light richly. I suppose he could have pinned the model with wire from above, snipped the wire, and let the house fall, burned out the tripod's shadow when printing. Or for menacing turbulence, cast shadows with pieces of cardboard, thrown dust in the air, or Venetian glitter (imported, fifty to eighty dollars an ounce) to get the effect of a storm approaching, that particular colloidal havoc. He might have filtered a tinge of green to deepen the sky. Learned, from a guy we both knew who grew up in Oklahoma, to view the storm-world from the belly of a ditch, to try that angle, and shoot the house as it pulley-and-levered by in a hail of marbles (Cat's Eyes, nineteen dollars a sack at Land of Marbles, in New York.)

There must be a thousand ways to make a thing seem to be a falling house, and the story behind it big.

Oh.

I get it. *Making-it-seem.*

No houses are falling.

The site isn't real. The crew isn't real.

Everything made is coming unmade.

Da Vinci—forgive me for harkening, of course it's unfair, out of step, out of line, a bit panicky, I know—Da Vinci drew the human body as if he were the body's creator, instructing us, once he himself perfected the gesture, about how, precisely when the arm extends, these muscles pull, and these wrap and cantilever bone. He wrote it all down, every move, to show the world—so hidden, so close—just below a flap a skin.

Or, put this way, Schiller wrote in "Ode to Joy," and of the poem itself, "this is my kiss to the world."

What must the artist think of us studying his catalog's photos of crews, the crane, the hard hats, the crowds assembling? Is he having a laugh? Is anyone laughing?

Am I missing any laughter here?

Isn't it good to laugh a little?

I'm looking up, as the artist suggests, into the blue, blue, blue of the photograph sky, and see there the green corner of a roof coming toward me. There's a sweetness to the green. A sadness to the falling.

If I know I've been led to believe a house is falling, can this picture still be an ode?

Can it constitute a song of praise, glorify a history, embody the broken, lost-forever, irretrievable bygone and frame it up against the clear sky?

Couldn't I go so far as to say here is our age's response to still-life, and sidle it up to the seventeenth century's Dutch flowers/fish/fruit picked and held precisely, lusciously up to the light, or against the high sheen of a gathering dark?

What is this note and tone of green pressed flat against the so-very blue?

Critique? Transgression?

Subversion, appropriation? Is this "terrain?" (Not, of course, real dusty ruts and vertiginous drop-offs, but nonetheless that which is meant to be rocky, uncharted?)

Here is a process, wherein we're meant to see something whole hoisted, dropped, and hoisted again until there's nothing left to lift and drop.

Is this playing like an elegy?

Am I feeling elegiac?

And don't the complications of this project (staging the sites, trussing the houses) have something to do with art's inherent artifice? (To go through all this to drop a house!)

Are these very questions the subject—heady, cloudy as they are—as others have chosen sinew and muscle and bone for their study?

Is it stupid to talk about Da Vinci, who bled animals dry, who pushed aside the yellow fat to slip his hands more deeply in, who drew quickly and, when not quickly enough, wore a mask to dull the scent?

Who drew with characteristic delicacy the most grotesque deformities. Who could lavish a wart. Caress a humpback.

Reread, now embraced by quotations marks, the following words four paragraphs above: "complications," "sites," "houses." I think you'll hear the particular laughter I was referring to earlier. Or at least an oscillation. Some tonal ether, some trickster wobble.

Or try these phrases I've made up, in catalogese:

"We speculate, yes, but are made to see only what the artist wants us to see...thus our unease, suspicion, doubt..." "...and that successful tension...charms, frustrates, cajoles." I haven't worked it out fully, but the words "indeterminate" and "mediate" would figure in somewhere.

I'm pretty sure these thoughts are obvious.

On Looking

But what of the feelings these images stir?

I know, I know...*feelings* and *stir.*

But I keep coming back to this spot of green. That's all, just the green, which, above all, holds me. It's of ripe avocados and hard young apples. Thin-skinned lake plants, as they float, cloud and wave. A curl of lime peel. New moss. Peridot, milked down with light. This simple-flat, sad-tender green, suspended against the broom-swept cirrus sky...

It's been a year now since she died.

Of all the green I make a stillness. Of sun-through-leaves, now, this June, I make a stillness. Of all the green, transparent spots I make a moment. I make a moment to hold her, and she falls, really falls, every time.

Glaciology

Plan

When the snow began to melt, the drifts left behind a surprising collection of junk—paper cups, socks, Matchbox trucks, a snarl of CAUTION-POLICE-CAUTION tape, pinkly wrapped tampons, oil-rag T-shirts, banana peels: intimacies of toy box, bathroom, and garage amid the lumps of sand and salt we threw down for traction. It was as if after the big event of snowfall we'd forgotten there was more, still, to be said. A cache of loose details below to attend. A trove poised. A stealth gathering.

Deposition below the singular-seeming white cover.

I shall make my own study of snow and time. I will learn from that which has built the very ground I'm now slipping around on: glaciers. Their formative act: deposition, for example: *fine grained rock debris, rock flour, and coarse rock fragments picked up or entrained within the base of a glacier and then transported and deposited from either active or stagnant ice. This product of glacial deposition, known as till, consists of particles that follow complicated routes, being deposited on the top or along the sides of the glacier bed, entrained again, and finally dropped. As a sediment, till has certain distinctive features: it exhibits poor sorting, is usually massive, and consists of large stones in a fine matrix of minerals and rock types.*

Poor sorting: I like that: that it all gets dropped, the big stuff enmeshed with the grainy soft stuff. The indiscriminate mess. That it forms a long train, so that seeing it all, one can trail events back. Guess at them. View time. And by way of the whole scattered and shifting pattern, by the gathering eye, make something of these loose details, collecting.

Deposition on Thaw

I will note, though its impetus was warmth, the sharpness of the thaw. During the thaw we were given to see the way snow melted into vertebrae, whole bodies of bone inclined toward one another. Bones stacked and bent in the attitude of prayer, the edges honed and precarious. Forms arced over the sewer grates and curbs as the gutter streamed with bubbly melt. What remained were not yet remains. It was clear how the warmth would eat everything down, but where some parts were colder than the rest, that core kept the figure upright. The shapes were knife-edged, hunched, easing a pain; they grayed and were everywhere pocked with dirt, and unlikely in their strength.

A few days later, just sheering, frayed patches covered the ground, and the elbows of everything poked through. White remained where the ground must have been colder, or wind blew and packed the snow hard.

How to read a land?

There were thicknesses, white places layered in smears that others were trained to read. *Densities* amid the rivulets of veins. *Occlusions. Artifacts.*

I remember, about the X-ray, thinking *Artifacts? That sounds harmless*. Evidence of some action passed—little shard, small bit taken out of my body and sent off for further study. Vase, mirror, tile. Lip of a cup. A thing that remained to be found and told. An image that sings about time.

Deposition on the Shapes of Tasks

Waiting all that long week—for test results, the snow to stop, dough to rise, nightfall—small tasks turned into days. Days unfolded into tasks. The inside-out arms of clothes pulled right, made whole and unwrinkled, took lovely hours. Tasks filled like balloons and rounded with breath; they floated and bumped around the day: some popcorn, some dishes, some mending. And though dressing for sledding, undressing, and draping everything wet over radiators was deliberate, a stitch ran through, jagged and taut, cinching the gestures tight with uncertainty. Everything coming down—snow, sleet, threat, delicacy—twined through like a rivulet, that cut water makes in its persistence, its pressure carving, so the bank grows a dangerous, fragile lip. The work of glaciers changes a landscape: old stream valleys are gouged and deepened, filled with till and outwash. *Filled,* of course, over millions of years. In sand-grain, fist-sized increments.

This kind of time illuminated tasks one would hardly be given to see otherwise. Titled them, even: the scraping of old wax from candlesticks; the tightening of loosened doorknobs. Oil-soaping the piano keys.

Deposition on Fevers and Still Lifes

That week time was ample, broad as a boulevard, a stroll, a meander. Not a tour. Not a map or a path to be found. School was canceled. Scents fully unfolded—coffee, chocolate, and milk marbling together on the stove, thinnest skin across to touch and lift and eat. And like a concentrate of heat itself, my bounded sight burned holes in the things most fixed upon: the ceiling's old butterfly water stain. One rough, gritty chip in the rim of a favorite cup.

It was in this way that joy and severity flared everywhere: along the banks of steep places I went to quickly, glanced, then ran from. They burned together in cornmeal in a pour, the yellow dust that rose and stuck to my hands as I folded in the unbeaten eggs, cold suns to poke and dim with flour—as outside, too, the cold sun dimmed, and the sky sifted and shushed down.

Yes, that week passed with a fever's disheveled clarity. That time, its atmosphere, moved the way fevers by turn dilute and intensify moments, so by evening one cannot reconstitute the day and calls it "lost," calls it "flown," says after a night's sleep "what happened to the day?" Things that week were touched in sweaty uncertainty and weakly released. There were intimacies akin to falling back to a pillow after water, soup, and tea were brought, gratitude unspoken; the night table's terrain, the book, the book's binding, glue at the binding and the word for each sewn section, *folio*, surfacing from far off. The sheet's silk piping to slip a finger idly under for coolness.

In its riotous stillness, that week was a study—Dutch, seventeenth century, with its controlled and ordered high flare and shine. Days held the light and feverish presence of a bowl of lemons in pocked disarray. Always one lemon pared in a spiral of undress, its inner skin gone a flushed, sweet-cream rose. Always the starry, cut sections browning and the darkness, just beyond the laden table, held almost successfully off. I, with my props—mixing bowl, dough—tilted toward, soaked in late afternoon light, while time raged all around in shadow, the dark stroking cup, quartered fig, plate of brilliant silver sardines left on the counter from lunch.

Deposition on Millennia/Effluvia

To say "a glacier formed this land" sanctifies the blink of an eye.

To see, from the air, glacial streams and think *like a snake* or *ribboning*, and of the land on either side *accordion* or *fan* colludes against awe. Neatens up the work of time. Makes of time a graven thing, hand-sculpted, carved, and held. Time should seize, should haul us back, then let go, wind-sheared into *now*, breathlessly into the moment's hard strata. Each morning in Rome, my old friend runs in a park along the aqueduct, which breaks and restarts in yellowed fields, its arches sprouting wild grasses, its arches collapsing, the houses, apartments, roads of his neighborhood visible through it—as houses and roads have been for nearly 2,000 years. You can sit on rocks in Central Park, soft outcrops undulant as sleeping bodies, formed tens of thousands of years ago and look up at the city skyline knowing the North American ice sheet flowed exactly that far south. Or hold in your hand a striated stone from Mauritania, abraded at the base of a glacier 650 million years ago, and touch the markings, those simple scratches so easily picked up and put down again on the touch-me table at the museum. Kick any stone beneath your foot, here, in Baltimore, and you're scuffing easily 300 million years of work.

I cast back for any one thing I did on any one day that week: how unencumbered the brushing of my hair, the perfect scrolls of carrot peel I lowered like a proclamation into the hamsters' cage; careless grace of understatement, luxury of simple gesture after gesture (fork to mouth, mouth to glass, fork and glass rinsed in the sink and—linger here, see the heat pulling fog up the glass, atilt and cooling in the drainboard). I'm calling up the tongue-and-groove gestures, the hook-and-eye moments of the day, so they might again spend themselves freely, mark the layers of events en route, classify the waiting. Cajoled from somewhere back in the morning, the peeling of that tangerine (cut thumb plunged into the yielding core, stinging and wet and red) comes forth.

I am recalling such occasions for attention offered in a day I was free to ignore. And now, am not free at all (for this *is* a deposition): cutting burnt crust away; snagging a sock on a rough stair plank; digging a sliver of dirt from a nail under running water. I am tied to the sight of the world, to things burnished and scoured by use, and by their diminution loved—as I so loved and saved my grandmother's wooden cooking spoon, older than me, smooth as driftwood, when to relieve her boredom, her aide used it to plant and prop a geranium on the balcony. The spoon has folded into its profile, has tucked within it, englaciated, the rim of the aluminum roasting pan (why that of all the nicked saucepans and ceramic bowls of creamy batters tapped and tapped and tapped against?). I took and washed (as my grandmother no longer can wash) its singed rack burns, its smooth neck, thinned from lifting huge roasts by their taut white lacings.

One idly picks up pine cones, rocks, shells to mark a moment, to commemorate time. One picks them up because they shine out from their mud, or water lapping brightens their veins and shorn faces, or there they are, wedged inexplicably whole in a jetty and a spiral tip beckons, though the center be partial and broken.

Deposition on Watches

That week my watch broke, so I borrowed my son's digital Monsters, Inc. watch. But I missed the clean, white face of my old one, and its circular sweep. The digital time dosed its minutes, shifted its numbers too economically one into the next, the angular 2 and angular 5 simple mirror images, a single bar across the middle making the 0 an 8. Then, as the days without school-time unwound and were lashed together instead by flares of fear, spots of love, solemn noon bell at the cathedral, all the morning's held breath, all the whites piling, like suds, their calm expanse up, it was easy to wear no watch at all. But I have not become a person divested of watches. I miss the circle's perpetuity, dawn and dusk sharing the same space, if only for minutes. The hour pinning itself to the changing light of seasons.

The watch I want now—I saw a picture of it yesterday—posits a looker at the center, who, to properly see the numbers, would have to turn and face each one: already by 2 the numbers start to tilt, so that the 6 is a 9, if you're outside looking in. But a 6 if you're in the middle. I like to think of standing in the center, arms reaching out and brushing all the minutes and hours.

I like the idea of turning to face the hour, having the hours arrayed around me. From a still point, having to face the increments of a day.

Deposition on Failure

Last May, I remember, on this very sidewalk: a fly's soap-bubble, gasoline colors; taut grimace on the face of a baby bird, that hatched and unliving, ancient, pimpled bud on the grass; corms of daylilies, and "corm" itself that most perfect union of "corn" and "worm," meaning exactly the thick, stubborn grub I hacked to separate. I remember the ripe, raw, shivery scents.

But during this thaw, come on so fast now— just for a day, just for caprice, it was sixty degrees.

And when I went out walking the sun was so soft—an assertion, bravura. Where warmth thawed the planes of bone like a high bank, my face was a running stream again. I took off my mittens and left them in the crook of a tree; it always takes a few days to believe the warmth.

The snow receded, the warmth returned, and I was fine. I was negative. *Negative, negative,* I was thinking, buoyant. The hard winter lifted all at once, the sun came, dewy and beading, the air was sweet and I was fine—oh burgeoning cliché I entertained, cannot believe I entertained: spring bearing its blood-tide and life all

97

abloom, all's well ending well in a spate, a thrall of undulant weather, etc. Rising, on cue, such music as dripping icicles conduct, such shine and promise, oh window of light on the nibbled Red Delicious little Sam just dropped. And the neighbors' voices carrying, the out-of-doors voices lofting, reconfiguring again the space between our houses: it was New World Symphony, English horn-solo-fresh. I was a turning season, a spit of land at low tide, a window thrown open. Would you believe it if I told you (told *unto* you, lo! for real) I saw a butterfly—and it was corn-yellow? I resisted the easy convergence— *spring, warmth, I'm fine*—not a bit, and I knew that to be an indulgence, a failure, partial sight. As if I had come to the brightness of that day wholly—wholly—from dark.

But I cannot forget—for this is a deposition—that all that dark week there was this, too: the diamond-blue light at each drift's core. My husband's abundant embrace. Sanctum of my child under quilts. In candlelight, sewing the ghost. Folding a swan. With books, in the folds of a story. Our son, himself, that most beloved unfolding.

And the color of the sky: workshirt-turned-inside-out, and the gray of our house against it, a darker inner seam, revealed. Our house an object light chose for lavishing, a river stone eddied into calm. The tender crack in a baking loaf, its creamy rift rough at the edges and going gold. Of all the names for snow considered, of all the shifts in tone it made, I found clamshell, bone, and pearl. That week I found lead in the white, mouse in it, and refracted granite. Talc with pepper. Layers of dried mud, zinc, and iron. Blown milkweed and ashy cinder. Silvered cornfield. Uncooked biscuit. Mummy, oatmeal, sand, and linen. Some morning glory. Some roadside aster.

Spires

I keep thinking of spires. How they must have appealed. That she might have wished for one to press her cheek to. I keep seeing rooftops, slate sharply pitched, as gray as high clouds, as a gathering storm. Smokestacks, the university's turrets, tram lines spoking out from the center of Warsaw, north toward the apartment we shared, ten years ago now. I keep seeing the city from air.

Ten years ago this All Souls' Day we took the train out to spend the afternoon with her family. It got dark very early. At the cemetery in Skierniewice, the candles, graveside, sent up a glow, a warm light without edges. There were so many people to push our way through. So much going on. The mums at each plot and the tidying up. The villagers with rakes and trowels and bags. Silk flowers, carnations, evergreen boughs. The newly-turned graves, their dark soil, wet. The picnics on graves, the deceased as host. Sitting down with the family, and the vodka brought out. Meat wrapped in paper and hunks of hard cheese. Pickles in jars. The blackberry jam. The plum wine and fruit brandies. Orange rinds in thick syrup. Sour tomatoes. Hardboiled eggs. The cabbage in spices, vinegar, salt. This return every year to keep company, faith. To keep solace going.

The church's thin spire against early night. The dark overtaking and honing the point. Filing it. Spire: the harder I looked for it, the more quickly it seemed to dissolve.

And after, back to her grandparents' farm. The lean-to with bathroom, coats hanging, and workboots. Inside, the kitchen's wood stove in a blaze. Soup going, and noodles. Walls stenciled with vines. Two small, high beds with crewel-work covers. Round tables with books, dried flowers, medicine. Steaming duck stew, blood sausage, pâtés, vegetable salads, brown bread, and more pickles. A hard bagel, blessed, and hung on a string along with the key to the wardrobe.

A spire. Ascent. A holy send-off. But the letter that came today said nothing of spires. Mentioned just an apartment. That she jumped from up there. Apartments in Warsaw are flat-roofed and blocky, each one like the next. Apartments are boxes and the stairs lead you up. We lived together like that. On weekends we'd hear the knife-grinder's bright bell as he wheeled his cart through the courtyard below. The long whine as he'd hold the blades to the stone. Then the noise growing faint as he pushed his cart on to the next courtyard and the next.

Once visiting her parents, hours from Warsaw, we heard it again, from up on their roof. I think it was something she always did—go up for the quiet, the solitude, even in winter. Go up to isolate one sound among many. Knife grinder. Train whistle. From the living room's balcony you could see—nothing. They hung their pheasants and quail out there, the meat so tender it fell from the bones and we picked shot from our mouths as we ate that night. Out there, the preserves and wrapped cheese stayed all winter. But you could see nothing. Just rows and rows of balconies piled with food and boxes and tools. So we went to the roof.

And from there we saw—nothing. From there, Skierniewice was

snow-patched and half-built. The stark land was flattened and scarred with trenches. The train station a blotch of coal smoke to the east. Kids crawling through drain pipes, kicking tangles of wire. Frozen tire-track humps, hardened in cold. Greasy puddles half-frozen, fumes heavy in air and the oil drums toppled. The dream of trees was years and years off. You walked past the blocks and blocks of apartments, not looking until you got to your door and then you ducked in and went up.

From the roof you could see, she said, the whole town. The whole blasted site. The scandal of progress, the terrible hope. Landscape of false starts. Of political whim, invisible funds. Of work on hold. The dirty paths scuffed from street to door. She said, *You can see the whole town from up here.* (But not the neat market square, miles off, no. Not the rough wooden tables abundant with oranges, beets, children's striped socks even in winter. Not the old, cobbled streets with cottages, yards, and small, resourceful, winterproofed gardens.)

She jumped from a roof, from forty floors up, two weeks before All Souls' Day. *A hard depression* her friend's letter said.

Up there was no spire, just flatness, blacktopped. Stubborn, decisive, she would have known this: a spire's a hook, a snag into light, a handhold, steadying. A stake in the sky, and she wanted none of it. She would go instead to a practical block, hunched on the earth. Modestly, to one with back stairs. I know how she climbed them—huffing and stopping to rest on the landing for only a second. Red-faced from the effort. We did it each day, going out, coming back: school, work, library, movie, museum. She'd have measured and thought the whole thing through, as she always thought through—anyone's sadness, disappointment, neglect. Birthdays. Occasions.

The street would be clear. She would carry ID.

She would not leave a note.

Ten years ago I sat at my window—reading and working, writing, translating, as she sat at hers across the hall. From there I could see young mothers with prams, sitting and chatting in the dry scruffy courtyard, their white breath gathering as they rebundled the children. I'd work and look out, work by looking—at nothing in particular: all the near balconies, tram cables, the highway, the bus lot that served as a market on Saturdays. Weigh and decide: this word or that one. Finish a line, go on to the next. I'd let the words come. I'd get up and come back, easing the distance between possibilities.

Once while I was working I looked up and saw a woman digging her window box out with a fork. It was cold. Late November. She dug and pulled the dry stalks up, shook the roots and put the old flower heads into a little basket. Then she hit a tough spot—it must have been frozen—and had to dig hard. The fork caught the plant's root and flipped it in air. She watched it go down. Put her hands on the rail and watched as it fell. Then she stopped altogether. Left the fork in. Left the window box like that, half-finished, all winter.

work by looking

(in memory, G. G.)

On Invisibility

I t is black and dull and coiled like excrement between the overturned boats. *Coiled like excrement*—that was the phrase, word for word, and then I read that D.H. Lawrence saw a snake in just that way. Exactly that.

I'll go on anyway.

Coiled like a rope dropped fast, coiled and dull as an arm after rowing, the slack muscle looped over bone and aching.

It's early fall and I am living for a while in the seam between weathers, with the whining of crickets and junketing locusts. A Viceroy dodges; the light spots on its wings are fine scales to sift the body through air. I move closer to the snake and it shifts, seeing me. *Overturn the stone of my heart*, I think. Being watched is something like being remade.

Later that day, I stand in the place the snake was coiled, where its jawbones unhinged to swallow a frog and, when finished, the single rough scale of its eyelid dropped down and made the moment dark. I stand in the place its body was. And the place is fearsome and thickened with presence. I say *God-fearing*, which I've never said, and mean by that *a trembling when walking on ground crosshatched by so many lives*. I mean *I fear being one of so many*.

Brown snake, barn snake, cow snake, no. "Common Water Snake" I read in the pocket guide, "vicious but not deadly." I like the honesty, the drama delivered as simple fact: what flashing and tearing, struggle and edge—and *recovery*—the guide's author observed to say that.

I stand in the place where a water snake rested. Between overturned boats with their rusting chains. On a bare spot of ground with tufted, dried grass.

And standing, I am stitched through by the hum and gather of wings on their way to a stand of cattails at edge of the lake.

When I step away the grass springs back, then straightens in sun. The world seals up and I am gone.

*

If the squirrels digging into our roof wore bells, we would hear them enter; then we could pound and scare them away before they got in. Barring that, *you got a friend with a BB gun?* the roofer asks. *Makes them go away real quick.*

*

A woman in a sprawling suburb nearby is angry about bears. They come into her yard and topple the garbage cans. One day her dog cornered a bear near the fence—*He did exactly as he was supposed to do to give us time to get away*, she says. But soon the bear wouldn't move at all; even as she banged on pots and yelled it wouldn't leave. The bear comes around often now and she's at the end of her rope. She wears a whistle all the time. Her kids can't play in the yard, for fear, and the dog is locked up. *Something's got to be done.*

On Looking

*

Make the bears invisible again. Invisible so that you must imagine: a bear once walked here, rocked this tree to shake down fruit before all the people moved into its space.

And fenced the apple. And planted peach.

Invisible: without a trace, kept out, planted over. *Unseen.*

There are so many ways: a trap as big as an oil drum. A gun. Bait, which lulls the bear to sleep. Something to stun. Bracelets and collars. Dogs and alarms.

*

In Bosch's hell, being unseen is a sickening constant: the action's all tripping, spilling, and cracking—all the bent bodies make a writhing mosaic—but no one is watching anyone else. If a tree were to fall in this forest of horrors there would be no philosophy, no koan about it— which requires the mind at nimble attention, human discussion, an idea in passing, passing along, gathering steam, gathering moss. And hell is being passed over untouched. Going glimpsed-but-unseen.

As happens anywhere, midafternoon. Or any time soft chairs are lined up, and the applause signs flash in the TV studio. And viewers in their own homes receive: the roars, the devouring, the language in filtered, monotonous bleeps. The music cued up and dramatically fading. *We hope that by bringing you the stories of these brave people you will be*—what, moved? educated? But first we will see, we will see and see: the stubby limbs, the mountains of flesh and crushed, cobbled ears, bodies pierced like St. Sebastian's, cruelty, fate, the huge boy's face filling the screen. And in the audience, the twisted relief on all the faces: *I am not he. Remember that,* the music says: remember, so gratitude grows and flowers, grows heavy and sweet with strange-shaped flowers, spiked and dripping. Flower-talons.

Ferocious, these toothy, untouchable flowers.

Remember the toddler as big as a bear—and his normal-sized mother and normal-sized aunt who spray their hair stiff and blink, silver-lidded, under the lights like the shutters of passé machines.

Framing us, whom they do not see.

*

I play the hand-over-hand game with my son. He is three. *What can I be when I am older?* (Anything you want.) *Maybe an artist and I can still live with you?* (Of course, of course.) We take turns hiding, revealing, and slapping our hands back down to the kitchen table. His hand is a weight and a fragility. Here and gone. For long, heavy months I was filled and waiting, and then, once I held him, the loss rushed in: first he will be here and then he will not. First he is with me—and then *I* am the fragility. Here and then gone. For now, we slap our hands down, faster and faster and pull them away, down and away, down and away. We make a blur of our hands and we laugh about it.

*

Once I looked in the mirror and saw—not a thing. So I made of my arm a sketchy ladder and climbed the pain up. I reeled myself into quietude. The pain was there, but the pain was good. It framed my body and held it still, until I could find myself again.

*

I walk down to the lake, to the spot under trees, to the open space between overturned boats again. In this dusty place, a water snake sat coiled in sun like a vine, like a belt, tense arm, long shadow, and (thought through the ages, not mine alone) *excrement*. I stay a

106

moment then slip away, quietly, that the snake might return, that it might be seen, oh let it be seen, dull, vicious, and coiled. Let it disgust and surprise someone else.

On Praise

My friend went down in a ditch of his own devising. A week later, dirty and stronger, he emerged, and we stood, none of us ditch-diggers, at the edge of the hole he made for a sewerline, like a route, from street to house. "Nice hole," the others said, but I was thinking how good it must have been, by this labor, to lower yourself into the ground to be held by the ground. How good, for a change, to stop and lean against the wall of your own work and measure with your body the achievement and the depth. With shoulders, keep even the width of the ditch. And resting, but not idly, take the earth between your fingers and roll your material to powder. Grind it between your teeth. Find it along the river of your spine.

I did not want to say, to have to say I was impressed—though for the sake of others standing and admiring, and convention, I agreed. No one digs his own ditch these days. But praise for your effort called up an emptiness. And hearing the word aloud, "impressed," an insufficiency. Because I know the way you work, stringing ligatures, stooping and rising with skeins and emulsions, with calipers of your own fashioning, cracking densities, minting and hoisting, probing and rowing toward. I know your precisely headlong way with undertakings: elsewhere, on a page. In a summer yard blackened with sour cherries. Photographing the cherries.

Praise referred not at all to the line you plotted, cast ahead, and kept in mind, descending. Praise could not reach the moment when, sticky and hot and pausing to drink, looking down at your hands gone chalky with dirt, they were anyone's hands. Praise called forth nothing about the stone in your shoe, kept in to sharpen, to pare a thought clean, to accompany so much methodical bending and lifting. Stone to refine the humidity. Stone of clarion pinch and private measure of resolve.

From the edge of the finished hole, looking in, I saw instead the story of your work: at the start, how shallow the roots of grass, and stubborn the mat of their underground twining. The way each new task required courting, appeared resistant, at first refused to unlock the sweet, rote place where the patterns are. You'd learn, by working, how a shovel favors one spot until you angle it away from the pull of the known. You'd find a way to concentrate force into essential gesture. There was stopping to dig around outcrops; stopping to pack and smooth the sides: decisions made with earth and body.

I could see the way the material, carefully attended, settled into coherence: by midday the ground resists; after rain there's slippage to skirt or shore up. At night, how many bricks (test wind, anticipate) to use to tack the sky-blue tarp.

And the rhythms found, each day, anew: *plunge and toss*, or *plunge and lift and toss*, two beats or three, according to the form's—your work's—requirement.

Proof that muscle compasses both rootedness and torque.

And there must have been songs—lines repeating, refrains cantilevering your swing. And, too, at rest after working all day, how the body goes on humming.

On Looking

I stood over your work and spoke a few words—though not because you required, instead of my silence, any affirmation. I admire the way you've routed that, almost, from your expectations, how it's nice when it comes, and desire for it flares, I know, but my praise didn't mean much, much after it was spoken, right? Because, better than that, being down in a hole, day after day, one learns the hydrostatic difference between 11:00 a.m. and 1:00 p.m. angles of light, and notes them, and works right through. Knowing nothing at first about the work before you, then finding the patterns it requires—that's what matters.

I know that about you.

And there was the slow rise or sharp clutch of gratitude—I'm guessing, but I think this is right—for the way a body keeps on strengthening. I'm sure there were long stretches of unencumbered joy in the arc and bend and heft of the heavy work, but better still, there was that paradox to hold: the ease of being strong and alive right up against the lousy habits you persist with, the damage you do, that, miracle, isn't more apparent in the body.

There would have been the shifting scents of uppermost dry, tufted browns gone to red and mustardy clays. Angles by which a tool comes to be known: the primary- and the relief-hold, and the smooth shifts between them so natural by the end of the week. And nicks in the blade—this from the first hard crack against quartz; this where you dulled the tip against the boxwood's roots. Blade worn like a pedal where you pushed with your boot. Dark stain on the wooden grip, salted by your hand.

We sit on your porch having a drink. Here, tilted into a corner, is your shovel. Now, weeks after the ditch has been filled, is hay-covered and settling, and your daughter runs right over it, laughing, you're thinking fast, fleet as the myth's terrible moment when the earth opens up and all the mortal bargaining begins. Here, gathered on the

111

porch with us, you're staying with that gash of a moment, you're holding, somewhere, a starkness few will let a moment turn to.

You're turning the moment in your hands, you're offering it so it breaks in the light and falls in shining disks and you harvest the disks, unseen, and again your hands are remade, and you fill your pockets and jingle the pockets.

Words for this are warming. Rolling between your fingers.

And how would the praise for that go: *"Good awe?" "Congrats?"*

For the well-tempered shock of being here, each clay-filled, light-plumbed moment ongoing, transparent, and loved: *"well done?"*

On Not Hurting a Fly:
A Memorial

*...fragments of cloth, bits of cotton, lumps of earth,
records of speech, pieces of wood and iron, phials of odors,
plates of food and excrement... a piece of the body torn
out by the root might be more to the point.*

—James Agee

I'd like to look at the issue seriously, since I've got a fly here and it's past being hurt; since, now that I'm looking, it's really a horsefly I smacked against the window weeks ago. A *horsefly*, which means I've stopped to ask questions. A horsefly, making the scene specific, just right for this discussion.

Why haven't I cleared it away? Like an old hurt or slight, it has softened and darkened, curled in upon itself. Small presence at the edge of sight, in a spot of sun. Sometimes when I'm working these days, deeply working, I'll glance down at my watch and see only ciphers, as if the numbers, worn smooth and blank as river stones, had nothing to do with time—or as much to do with it as the grainy whorls in this desk, distant, unreadable now. I go back to work, head bent, caught up in the moment, unmarked.

In the past few weeks I've overlooked the fly as if it, too, were a cipher, a nick in the sill, or a small, indigenous dropped thing: an acorn, a seed pod half-hidden in brush. I've grown accustomed to it, just off to the side, bent into the shape of a comma, half-stasis, brief pause before continuing on.

Here is a joke: a priest, a minister, and a rabbi are asked what they would hope to hear at their funerals. The priest hopes to learn he was a spiritual leader of great comfort to his parishioners; the minister hopes it might be said that he inspired many to a life of service and godliness. The rabbi, when asked, hopes someone will say "Hey, wait! I think I saw him move!"

Sometimes, out of the corner of my eye, I think I see the fly move. Even after so many weeks. Because its body remains, I startle first and ask questions later. Because the fly has grown porous by now, and brittle, the softest breeze sifts its papery wings. The air, passing over like a gaze, enlivens, inhabits, suggests.

This summer I met someone who kept a jar of dead flies on his porch. Whenever he found one he put it in; it took only a month or so to fill the jar completely up. He's a remarkable person who had a frightening childhood—though I doubt this has anything to do with the flies. He just seems to like clean, uncluttered surroundings. I want to emphasize again that he doesn't kill the flies and isn't trying to build a collection. But there they were on the little table, contained and ready for easy observation, the jar organizational, a place to keep things-of-a-kind as he kept papers filed, books neatly stacked. By midsummer when the jar was full, the bodies were beginning to compact, the whole mass settling like a snarl of hair. I wondered what the effect of a jar of dragonflies would be, the lace of their wings complicating the scene, making the ravaging more useless still. Why crush, even in death, the dragonfly that eats mosquitoes, gnats, and moths and does not bite us? Whose head is nearly covered with eyes, whose wings are sheer, as fragile as tatting, and beat a hundred times a second. Whose body is emerald, periwinkle, cobalt—electric colors of a falling sky.

(Though of course the bumblebee, too, is beautiful: ample and furred. And cicadas are airborne, humming spectra. And aphids weigh not even a breath, and potato beetles outshine anthracite in sun....)

Have you heard this before: war does not kill thousands of people; one person dies thousands of times?

That at last count there were 59,939 names engraved on the Vietnam War Memorial in Washington, D.C.?

I've always been puzzled by the phrase "She wouldn't hurt a fly." It never-minds the effort required to actually swat a fly, and moreover, the fly becomes a wee, small thing to which no harm should come. Speaking the words, one suspends one's feelings about the fly—a droning, disease-carrying, nerve-rattling pest. Meaning fractures. The fly stands in for "a thing not to be hurt," corresponds not at all to our perception.

That is, we disembody it.

I have a friend who won't swat even mosquitoes, though he, too, gets bitten. It's as if his capacity for annoyance has simply run out, or perhaps he has run it out of his body. He focuses a placid eye on the world, exists in quiet brotherhood with all things and so mosquitoes don't distract him any more than the bitter cold of winter and heat of summer he works through, doing all kinds of jobs. He drives a pickup truck all over town. Once I found a chipmunk he hit and killed on the road.

And so, because of what his regret would be; because the animal was completely flattened, its body a pool for ants in the heat; because I will never tell him I saw the eyes aligned on a single plane, the mouth open and grains of teeth pressed like a zipper into the earth;

115

for the time it takes to see the things in front of me; for the whorls in the table I work on, for the nicks and gouges, rings and years, erasures and grime—I will look again at the fly on the sill:

its three-part body. Its pair of wings and sets of legs—six haired legs that end in claws—attached to the center segment. Its shovel-like mouthparts. Its hard outer covering. A black that, back-lit at the end of the day, is flecked with furred gold. Enormous, multiple eyes-in-a-grid the size of its head (I used a magnifying glass) and the hair-like antennae between its eyes.

I am following the body back to itself. From mouthpart to head, down-sloping to wings, my looking moves moebus-like over the joints and segments, the sharp parts, the soft transparencies.

The wings askew. The missing leg.

And though I failed to see it at first, *thanks* now to the body, its constancy. Though I let it wait and it waited, dependable matter. Thanks to the wings, which are gently veined like a fine pen drawing of tributaries. Thanks to the bead of its head, the bristles and faceted eyes like velvet. Thanks to the body for permitting return to what I once knew urgently:

her body is mine. 1972. I saw the burning girl, stilled on TV, motionless, running, running and crying, and knew that was me in Vietnam. I knew as I ran to the kitchen and pressed my face to the cool, pearly snaps on my mother's jeans as she washed the dishes, and I couldn't speak—I knew I was burning on TV. The flames were behind me, were black and white and I was stilled and I was running, my clothes gone and it was snowing on TV, though it was summer and I was breathless and sweating.

That was Kim Phuc and we were almost nine years old.

I'm following the body.

At the Vietnam War Memorial my finger traces, from my hometown, *Howard Martin Gerstel.* That stands for his body. (*Jewish,*

On Looking

Married, I look up. *Casualty Type: Hostile, Gun, Small Arms Fire, Ground Casualty.*) I loop around the letters...I was three when he was killed. I was four when Robert George Hufschmid, also from my town, *Married, Catholic,* died: *Hostile, Artillery Rocket, Mortar, Ground Casualty.* Four when my uncle, in the Peace Corps instead, raising chickens in southern India, nearly died of measles. I ask him about the year, exactly, because my son is four now. Because his body is still of my body, and we go on like this, daily, my arms containing the smallness he makes of himself when he curls in my lap. My arms around him, bracketing him, enclosing the ribs and the taut, delicate skin between them. Though I know it will not go on like this always.

"It goes on," I say, *"forever,"* when I first see the wall. But it's not forever and I am annoyed at my own hyperbole. It's only enormous, a cut, polished edge that holds the earth back. The wall starts in the ground, reaches an apex and narrows down, something like an open book propped on the belly of earth. As we pass, our bodies are reflected in the black, buffed surface. It looks like a printer's case gone wild, kicked and reset, as the eye blurs over so many names. There are the ancient ones: Ham. Abel. Isaiah. Behind the memorial, maples reach with their colors; it's a bright November day. The names rise above our heads as we walk down, down imperceptibly, as if into a tomb. Visitors rub the names onto paper the concession guys give out for free. Circle the names with their fingers and hands, sit and stare and tell their stories. Tell their kids "Hal commanded D company." Israel. Samuel. And as you ascend, the names trickle to a close at the wall's far point. The names of the dead are the names of the living and in that way, too, go on: Herrera, my friend in California. Figueroa, my friend in New York. Carotenuto, my student. Boudreau, my old art teacher. Schwartzkopf. Kennedy. Abraham. Jeremiah. People take pictures of everything, even the phonebook-sized map of the names' locations, home towns, and dates of death. Therein are the places of my life, too: Hewlett, Oberlin, Iowa City, Baltimore. It takes me no time to find my birthday, and it is no one's death day.

117

The pamphlet I picked up says "By virtue of its design, the memorial puts a human face on a divisive conflict."

But there are no faces here at all. Or the faces are fleet, sheerest outlines we conjure back into mind. Private faces. Singular faces. Except as metaphor, war—conflict—does not wear a face.

Yes, stories come back.

Stories kindle forth a moment.

But that's not the body.

And neither are the figurative women, bronzed, in the Women's Vietnam Memorial, bodies. They are larger than life, in the posture of *tending*. *Pained* by the soldiers in their arms, dying. They lean like italics into the virtues they mean to portray: *bravery, duty, compassion*.

But that's not the body.

Nor do the bodies rising out of the flames of the Katyn Memorial burn like bodies. In Baltimore, at President Street and Aliceanna, the Polish soldiers climb flames like stepstools, their gilded forms lofted, on righteousness, up. The fire itself is sturdy and trusted; it becomes the men's legs and thus they are "enduring in memory," and mean to show the spirit unbroken. The spirit rising.

But this is not the body in flames.

And in the Tomb of the Unknown Soldier, even the bones themselves are not the body. Are a portion standing in for the whole, synecdoche, not meant to be Michael J. Blassie, shot down in An Loc in 1972. Though it is he, the DNA test now tells us. Unequivocally. But the medal of honor, though it hung over him for fourteen years, does not, it was ruled, belong to him.

He just lent his body to an idea.

"We really believe the medal should follow Michael," said Captain Patricia Blassie of the Air Force, his sister.

But it can't. It must not be allowed to attach to a body. Must remain: clean. Rapturous. Dignified.

In perpetual anonymity.

On Looking

———

The titles of Goya's etchings in *The Disasters of War* are amazingly simple. #22—"All This and More." #23—"The Same Thing Elsewhere." #37—"This Is Worse." And here, I stop. Soldiers rest in a grove of trees, but nearby, impaled on a jagged stump, as partial and perfect as any Greek statue: his body, his shapely calf, the shadings of thigh and muscled back and, filling the space where his forearm was hacked, a darkness in the background flowering.

I did not know a man could grow from a tree, until I saw precisely how.

I did not know the ways, precisely, a neck goes taut with fear, until *Guernica*. Did not know a mouth, uptilted as simply as a cup, could fill so easily with black cries, or the many ways animals could scream. That growing from a neck, a leg can arc around and pierce the neck; a kneecap weigh so much upon escape it drags along the floor, or breasts go sharp. That triangles spurt. That from the hilt of a sword a twisted flower might grow like a mangled fist.

Mississippi. 1954. Emmett Till, fourteen, is murdered for whistling at a white woman in a store, his body thrown into the Tallahatchie River. "All beating was concentrated around his head," said his mother, Mamie Till Mobley, describing the body when it was returned to her in its coffin. "It looked as if they had taken a nut-picker and picked the left eye out. The right eye was about mid-way to his cheek, his nose looked like they had taken a meat chopper and just chopped along the bridge of the nose. Where they tied that gin fan around his neck, the weight of it had choked his tongue out. I did not know a human tongue was so big."

His nickname was Bobo.

His face was strip-mined. A ditchful of flux. A pile of slag.

A sand dune sliding. A plate of meat. Mushrooms in a field of rain.

119

I was not yet born at the time, so I looked up the face in *Jet Magazine*.

At the funeral, the coffin was kept open. His mother said she "wanted the world to see what they did to my boy."

Da Vinci flayed the human body to better understand, to draw "sweet fleshiness with simple folds and roundness of limbs." "Do not" he said, "make all the muscles of your figures apparent... limbs which are not in exercise must be drawn without showing the play of muscles. And if you do otherwise, you will have imitated a bag of nuts rather than a human figure."

I did not know muscles wrapped in bands from chest to shoulder, tucked into the upper arm and folded under. That below the sinews and tendons, muscles were strapped like the staves of a basket across the chest. Until I went to see how autopsies are done, I did not know how small and pale the stomach was, that empty lungs are not light but will flop like fins when turned over, the two-lobed right one and the three-lobed left. That intercostal veins thread through the chest like perfectly basted hems. The epiglottis purses like the lip of a pitcher, and when the pituitary gland is lifted free of the brain it pops out with a neat little sound.

Fat is so yellow.

Veins are not blue but a soft, pearly gray.

A memorial can happen anywhere.

As it did, just recently, at a friend's farm. I was walking through the yellow-brown stubble in early fall, after the last hay was cut, when I saw a deer. It was curled in a grassy depression just before a stand of trees. The deer was so small that I startled, thinking it was sleeping in a little nest. But when I moved toward it, it didn't stir and I saw near the jaw a quarter-sized hole. The body was perfect except for the hole, which was terribly precise. The hole was deep, and the blood hadn't slipped in runnels all over but dried black at the rim. I had never seen a deer that close. So I stayed.

I circled around again. On one side, the body was perfect, but then on the other, when I crossed over, there was the hole come upon like disbelief, the perfect jawbone pierced through, collapsed in. The hole like a cave. Like a cup. Like an ear, half-drowned and mud-filled. The darkness there was seeping pink. The pink underneath was—I couldn't tell what. So I stayed with the body. So I kept looking in.

On Looking Away:
A Panoramic

Once I saw:

at an exhibition, balanced on its points, a blowfish, inflated, shellacked. Its empty stomach was mottled pink, brown, and cream. Its mouth was open, the lips a thin, stretched O of surprise. So easy someone had made it to forget the working insides, to forget, so we might tilt toward the light a hollow balloon of pleasure. Dip safely a finger into the spaces between flared needles.

And once...

But it wasn't just once. There are so many things to consider looking away from.

Once an emerald dragonfly landed in front of me on a cashier's thin arm. Its jittery sheen articulated as she moved and made her smaller by that trick, partial, and barely seen.

Tattoos are sad things. So one-time-only. The need to be marked so openly displayed and then, well, that little picture is all you get.

And how much the poor image is meant to hold: such a record of need, all painstaking decision or quick impetuousness recorded on the skin. The snapshot of the big event and not the big event itself (the one that lives behind the skin, always, always unseen) makes anyone forever the guy with his old war stories. About Johnnie. Remember him? True love you had for that guy. Like a brother...wife gave me his medal.... Heraldry, desire, homage crushed down to shamrock, Tasmanian devil, or, demurely—let's not go too far, let's not go crazy—a sweet-pea vine at the ankle. Muted registers, in case of disappointment. Muted regions of the body, in case of having-to-learn-to-live-with.

Once I saw them.

But how that came to be involves a complicated set of strategies, the history of our own Office of War Information, a break with the Geneva Conventions. I saw the bloated faces of the evil tyrant's sons. Browned. Potatoed. Like things hauled from saltwater. It must be that proof is dilatory, elastic, as expansive as the very early morning hours devoted to a single task. After all, "It is not a practice the United States engages in on a normal basis" said Secretary of State Donald Rumsfeld. And "I honestly believe that these two are particularly bad characters, and that it's important for the Iraqi people to see them, to know they're gone, to know they're dead and to know they're not coming back." For *this* purpose the faces are shown, for the purpose of indentifying monsters. For surely monsters look like monsters—see? Enduringly. And as surely, there is a child in bed, insistent, *but, but-ing* in the buttery light of happy endings: *what about the troll/witch/dragon—are they really dead?* Surely there is a mother imposing *sleep now, shhhh.* (And surely, the child—didn't you?—gathers the loose threads of the story into her hand, since threads show in even the best stories, and asks: *what happened to the beanstalk after?* And: *did they eat the witch they kicked into the oven?*

On Looking

And: *aren't there more witches out there? I know this story goes on,* thinks the child....)

Once I saw her.

But then, just like that, the next summer she was gone. When I called the director of the state fair, his secretary told me that people complained and said she was inappropriate and was being exploited. In her air-conditioned trailer with her newspaper and knitting, sitting, tiny legs crossed, tiny bonnet of blue calico and little calico apron kindling questions (how old *is* she? is she from this century? were, maybe, people smaller then?). The seat a little too high, just an inch, so her feet would dangle, making her even more specimenlike. Polite yet brief about the questions. Oh, she was a lovely person, and she liked her work and chose to do it, the state fair director's secretary told me. Velvet rope between her and the quiet people filing by. Nothing about her left you exactly breathless. Gravitational issues though: the onlookers' sudden, unexpected shame, embarrassment—no clue that this would happen—like entering a river, and suddenly the river is alive, minnows uncomfortably nibbling at toes, the current tugging. Soon an iciness not at all refreshing.

Most everyone hurried through.

One might resist:

touching a chicken to clean it, and retreat from its smallness and loose, bumpy skin where once feathers were and were scalded off. One might refuse the articulated movement of its legs while washing it under the water in the sink and still eat the chicken. Cooked by another: *Mediterranean. Fantastique.* Wined and buttered breast and thigh and leg transformed. Under pineapple, so you don't have to see. And can finally eat.

———

125

Lia Purpura

One might resist:

the article about a mother, hot water, steel wool, her child. One might resist the phrase "her child." One might start to read, and knowing at once what's coming, seeing where it's going *(bathtub, peroxide, wound,* and *squirt)* turn away. Feel the sheer drop-off, the height scaled fast and the sharp rocks shift underfoot. One might keep the article, file it, because all around the air is thinning. Because such helplessness splinters anyone. If you're not a mother, or a father, you don't know what it's like to want—and maybe only once, and maybe only glancingly—to do anything, anything to make the crying stop, to stop your own helplessness in the face of it. How, even if only for a moment, you feel broken apart. And that's when the shards start flying.

Remember the last time you had a speck in the eye? How you could think of nothing else?

But you closed your eyes to stop the irritation.

But you took a deep breath and the moment passed.

Right?

Here is a boy whose eye could be fixed. In the West. In America. But in the photo it's slipping inward. And here is his mother whose black, body-long burqa, when she squats, makes her look like a mountain. A mountain of slag from a freshly dug ditch. Whose entire face is covered with meshing. Here is a mother whose eyes are graphed, whose cheek is graphed when he flies to her and presses hard for a kiss. What is a kiss through mesh—a graphed breath? Here is a mother who cannot find the eyes of her son. Here is a boy with a mountain for a mother. A newspaper lays these things before you, at your feet—good dog—in black and white, and black and white allows the incremental 1-2-3 of understanding. A reader says I see, I see. Then leaves. For orange juice. Water. Small pleasures/ consolations of tea.

126

On Looking

If I am going to stay with these children (the girl's name is Sylena), I have to consider what they turn towards. Heliotropically. Tiny, back-bent supplicants searching under beds, around corners: *Mom, where are you?* Child-as-heliostat fixed to reflect the sun's rays, continuously, even as the sun turns away. And heliotropes: any kind of small, reddish-purple flower from Heliopolis, city of ruins, ruined, with a modern city superimposed, oh site of hurry and bustle, with ghost words and echoes, our ears too dulled to gauge a cry—of protest? exhaustion? hunger rising? And here, still standing in the city, my city, the story of the terrible bathtub, the story a reader might choose—*I* chose, because I am on trial here—to pass over one recent morning, to concentrate instead on the interesting demolition, 10th Avenue, the whole west side of the building torn off, the rooms like holes, empty, except for one.

With a white bathtub.

That stops me.

Ladder built back to the scene I keep turning away from.

The tub is clean. Very clean of the bodies (her body) (Sylena's) (and the soaps and towels heaped on the floor would have been wet, and worse). (And here comes the wet bed that the child didn't, didn't mean to, that I couldn't, I cannot . . . fix, clean. Fold away.)

And look! There are Murphy beds, still, in this part of town. See them in the torn up apartments! Remember the velvet ropes across the rooms in the Tenement Museum and the Murphy beds there. I remember that . . . safely now. I'm safe for now.

I paid my admission.

Then this comes:

How would all the tenement children live in just two rooms?

Crammed, I suppose. Crammed into, like these specimens I'm here to see, I'm not turning away from. Here in the museum of things gone terribly wrong, the Mütter Museum of Medical

127

Lia Purpura

Oddities, in Philadelphia. All the specimens: a loud carbuncle in plaster, on the back of a neck, like a scream. A smallpox pustule like an open mouth, its lips pulled down in sorrow in the photograph. The (forgive me) macaroni & cheese-with-ketchup face of a syphilitic. The gorgeous phrase "cavity of the sacrum" followed by photos of Frederik Ruysch's tiny, mounted fetal skeletons, some playing miniature bone-and-ligament violins, some jarred and injected with wax, talc, cinnabar, oil of lavendar, alcohol, black pepper, colored pigments to better illustrate the transcience of life and other allegorical lessons. And some he draped with embroidered lace. And to some he gave a mesentery handkerchief to accompany postures of grief.

The word *caries*. The words *phial* and *lancet* and *paregoric*. And *mercury pastille*.

One fetus—like Da Vinci's Hyperion Man, limbs out to measure the breadth of the known universe with its body—is really one star of conjoined twins, a head at either end and arms and legs as shining points. A star in the process of exploding, but caught. A star that didn't explode at all. Among such pinkness and tension and sadness, among the weightless beings strung up and clamped to best show their features, heads bent below a meniscus of poison, heads cresting the terrible solutions—I sat down. I stepped into their sleep.

And when I peered around to see their open backs, where the seam of them split, and the heat clanked on in the ancient radiators, and a toilet somewhere loudly flushed and the lobby voices were pistons churning the room...what was the difference, *sitting with?*

I read the medieval explanation about these bodies: God's anger. The Devil's hand at work. Some fear, danger, tragedy striking a mother straight through to her child. I looked and looked past reason to the useless necks again. To *sit with* you have to look into the gap in your understanding, not drive the conversation, not know where it's going. Not know beforehand at all where it's heading. I

128

read once, *there is a quality of legend about freaks... like a person in a fairy tale who stops and demands that you answer a riddle.* That's the space. That open field, where you're sitting with, and don't have the answer, but an atmosphere of response is forming.

I'm reading about a death-row inmate called "Little Lew." And though here he is, framed in his neat newspaper photo, he is hard to see for all his running—away from home at seven, then a little blur escaping from juvenile detention. Little Lew, who, by twelve, was already a father. (He's flying now.) Who loved guns from early on ("I can't even explain why. Just had to have one."). At 5'3" and 117 pounds, he's feather-blown. Of his weight, say *Welter:* "to roll," "to roll about, as in mud," and used figuratively as in: "they weltered in sin." "To be soaked, stained or bathed," as in: "the corpses weltered in their own blood." As in: "Leoma Chmielewski," after Lew shot her in the face during a robbery.

It took nine corrections officers to hold him down while the IV tubes were inserted in his arms.

The prisons' chief said he would have preferred not to have cameras involved in the execution process.

Of the drugs used to anesthetize, paralyze, and kill (sodium pentothal, pancuronium bromide, and potassium chloride), the first, the article states, can mask symptoms of an agonizing death by suffocation. It's banned by the American Veterinary Medical Association.

There were no signs that Williams suffered "once his struggles ceased" the article continues. "But that does not mean he did not feel pain" the article also reads.

Little kids playing hide-and-seek close their eyes and suppose no one can see them.

Safe, safe, safe.

Here's Little Lew's little picture, stamp-sized on page 1 of the paper. Below it *See Killer p. A2, Columbus Dispatch*, no picture, just words. But I see him there. I see him and see him. He is an argument hanging in air. He is a memory no one wants. He's stubborn. Little Lew who ran away keeps turning up unannounced. Shoots the face off my peace right now.

Right now I was sketching his face, the mustache and beard that encircled his open mouth. Two easy concentricities, my favorite design to draw. One circle inside another. It's on the necklace I wear, a lozenge of silver with a bronze washer soldered on. I believe in the circle. Small circle on a larger one, my child always with me that way.

I also collect washers I find in the street. You'd be surprised at how many there are to be found. I have three already from Columbus, Ohio, where I'm living for a few weeks. At home I have small pea-sized ones, and large ones I can barely palm. Pocked, rusty, and scratched; smooth and bright. Lots from Baltimore and from New York. Sometimes I think I should catalog them with little tags and note the circumstances under which they were found. One has a raised pattern like a prayer ring, a chaplet, whose bumps you thumb along while reciting your Our Fathers and Hail Marys. One is black; one is toothed like a kid's sketch of the sun. Easy to slide into my little mania. Even a friend of mine looks for them now. He finds them everywhere, though it took him a while to see them. I told him he had to train his eye for the object he desired, to practice being alert for the shape and sudden shine. And then they would come to him.

Two weeks after Lew was executed, another man lay strapped to the same gurney. The *Columbus Dispatch* reported that it took a team of prison health workers twenty minutes to find the veins on murderer John Glen Roe and to insert the shunts that would hold the needles carrying the lethal drugs. Family members of his victim, Donette Crawford, held hands and watched the execution on closed-circuit TV.

And where did they go after that? After the warden announced he was dead and Donette's sister, Michelle, raised up the hands of her father and sister's fiancé and said "Yes." After they saw the last breath, and were certain he was gone—where did they go? At 10:24 in the morning—out to breakfast? For a walk? To the cemetery? Where do you go and what do you do after watching an execution?

Here's another scene about staying to see:

Once I wanted to squat down and be with the yellows and greens and trace the U of a crushed frog's jawline. Its missing belly was a washed-out place. The middle was a smear, a wetness in the ease of light rain. And then its legs picked up again. Bent close to it, I wanted to sing aloud the song in my head, "Everyday is Like Sunday," and it could've been Sunday when this happened, it was still fresh. I was looking for its hand, the longer index finger and little thumb (I'll call them "hand," "finger" and "thumb") pressed white to the bone on the blue asphalt. Why stand over it? Why want to stay if the day is so joyously unfolding? The frog was all mouth. The crush opened and spread it and made it as wide as the day was wide. But I was dragged away. I had plans, a talk to give. Spring air, rain, all the bodies filing into the auditorium—I wanted to stay, but there was so much going on. Only now can I return to it. The yellows and greens and reds gone pink in the rain and spreading. Some brown from tires, and the treads evident. The sky was uncolored and *silent and gray*, the song was saying. But the frog wasn't silent and gray. Not at all.

And another:

At the El Greco show at the Met, the paintings soar because they are huge and because the figures themselves are so radically elongated. I'm finally face to face with the one I've been searching for, the one I've known since I was a child, looking through my parents' art books, "St. Martin and the Beggar." And because the painting is so large, I'm eye to eye with the beggar's hands, his terribly, painfully long, knobbed knuckles. And the others, too, gathered around it comment on his hands. And isn't this the way children go about looking, those for whom such attention is sanctioned, for whom finding is daily, who state simply, aloud, or pose as a question: *why are his knuckles so long?* Travel up the ripple of the beggar's arm to St. Martin's silver armor and over his white-rumped horse into the gray sky behind them. Travel up the leg of the beggar, bent unnaturally in at the knee, the effect lengthening the foot. You come to it, bring all your desire to the painting because you seek in it a mood, a sensation. So that you can say, by way of sight, "the beggar, pained and cold, is receiving a portion of St. Martin's cloak," and be in the presence of something unspeakable, by way of the the unnatural bend of the body, the graying and bluing of the body, which is part agony, part beauty.

And this one, occuring on a day like any other day:

Days after the photo of an Iraqi prisoner is released, the famous one where he is made to stand on a box with wires attached to his hands, black hood on his head and black cloak over his body (he was told not to move or he'd be electrocuted), I walk past a church in Bolton Hill, in Baltimore, on the north side of which is a Tiffany stained-glass Christ in flowing robes. The leaded panes emanate from Christ's hands, his body inclines toward the street, bending, as if to whisper to me. And the superimposition rises. The images converge. It's the spring of 2004, and I will be able to say this in America and know, reader, you, too, will have seen the hooded prisoner. First the words: *is he not Christ?* about the prisoner come. Then—though I am not Christian—all those who inhabit Christ's body populate the glass, and it lights, and the wash of light is suddenly made of motes, of little sharpened points, of heads and bodies like small fists, upthrust. Christ has found the prisoner's posture, Christ took it on. Or always knew. And since I have seen, since Christ looked into me—what a prisoner I must be. Or speck. Or mote. Or single light.

On Looking

What to say in a situation like this, when seeing, you are unexpectedly seen?

Once I saw something that could've been a horror but wasn't—my friend's arm around his daughter, first at rest on the small of her back, then wrapping further to make a full circle. It was beautiful. Loving. There was no swarm of bees in the girl's stomach. I didn't have to see, in her place, that other girl, too big on a man's lap, on the bus in Warsaw, being "dandled"—awful word that came to me and was everafter poisoned—and try, in a language I hardly spoke, to say "stop." I didn't have to see, for once, as a mother and leap up. Or remember anything with my body.

I look away. And if she's still there, and she is, the girl in the bathtub, the girl in the article held by the words, and her name is Sylena—if I look away and she is still there, then I am not free.

How to stay with her? As if with the dying, by way of a vigil, which is to form, with others, a house of shelter, to make a green respite, a *hospice*, a place a traveler might rest while passing though? I watched the sun at the window over the—how strange the precision while my friend was dying—*cafe curtains*. The cool June afternoon resounded with, only once but loudly, a car alarm, and neighbors' voices. I watched from the foot of the bed past the boxes of meds and the useless hundreds of vitamin bottles, and didn't turn away from the moment of passing, though it was more like a ceasing. Because nothing stepped forth in the form of announcement, no herald. The light was just part of the branches scratching, and the scratching bore no message. It was June 24th. I did not turn away. The knob of the bed was an anchor, burnished. Like—may I veer, just briefly here?—the bare breasts on the statue of the muse on 33rd and Charles Street, her bronze breasts shining from touch, from men late at night, boys after school just touching for luck, and why not, walking

133

with buddies and laughing, everyone does, it's just a moment to be alive. So alive.

The bedposts were mahogany and they shone too, from years and years of touching.

In Tod Browning's film, *Freaks,* the side-show performers "live by a code unto themselves," says the narrator at the begining. The pinheads, the dwarfs, the bearded woman, the worm-man in a sack, the Siamese twins live in a camp in their carved and painted folksy caravans. The interesting tension in the film is between the arc of the story line and the viewer's desire to see the freaks, to be allowed to see and not have to turn away, a kind of sanctioned privacy. The camera lingers over them and gives each the space to perform his or her own calling-card trick or accomplishment. The woman who used her feet as deftly as hands. The limbless man who moved like a worm and who rolled his own cigarettes with his teeth and struck a match and smoked. Beyond this, we are aware of waiting for *something* to happen. And it does. All the freaks, seeking revenge on the duplicitous "normal" performer, assemble under a rickety caravan to launch their attack; it's raining, the freaks are crawling on their bellies in the mud toward the beautiful/evil one to do her in. But then, they all fall together in a crumple and each of them is lost to the pile, and their singularity, yes, their *nobility,* dissolves.

Once there was a green elephant and a purple elephant and they lived in a house together. The house and the elephants were part of a old German children's game I played with at my grandmother's house. They lived together in other ways, as shapes and textures, quite aside from being elephants, and now they come back to me as the pleasure of colors paired up in the garden world of alysum and lavender, purple aster and moss. The elephants sat squatly with their fat legs out in front and stomachs curved over. And the little wrinkles in their trunks were nice elephant touches. They were made of soapstone and were nicked with fingernail scratches. But they lived as colors best.

Today, purple calls sun down to light the soft green of thyme, undried and fuzzily growing. Green and purple pair themselves so the eye might gather on clover, lamb's ear, morning glory.

What did the colors do to my eye?

Not once have I forgotten that the elephants were contorted, stubby, disproportionate.

Reader, I finished the article. About Sylena.

When I finished I had an inkling about a word. The word *strafe* came forth, unbidden. I looked it up for confirmation: *to punish. To reprimand viciously. From the German.*

What did I see, after I read? After I read, I stared out at the backyard and made a calming list: apple tree, loblolly, morning glory, ash. Rose-of-Sharon, tiger lily. 1-2-3 of black telephone wires against the blue sky, the Every Good Boy (Does Fine) for the invisible notes to climb. Checked the porthole of leaves that lets me see through to the next street. Sunk a bit into the deep brown of the shed. Opened the window a little for breeze.

What did I see while reading?

That once I used steel wool as a ball of tinsel in a pinch.

That when I said *fuck you* to my great aunt, and she washed my mouth out with soap (as soap occurred in the article, too), I studied the scratches in the very dull, very clean silver spiggots and, so close, saw the green spot where a drip wore the porcelain away.

Such focus made me dizzy, even then. "Custody of the eyes," my friend, a former nun tells me, is the practice of training your sight to focus only on the meditation, task, prayer in front of you, and you let nothing else in. But what if the object in front of you swims, dares swim away?

Lia Purpura

I will tell you a silver spiggot can swim. And the sky be white. And a faucet bear a hurricane.

I focused on the green porcelain spot as if it were the sun. I found I could make it be many pictures—a mossy rock, a turtle's back. But I tried to keep it the sun. I was maybe eight at the time.

Even then I focused hard.

I felt I might be tested on the things I saw.

NOTES

"Autopsy Report": . . . *the silent part of my life as a child* is from Virginia Woolf's essay "A Sketch of the Past."

"On Form": some italicized lines are from various poems of Gerard Manley Hopkins.

"Recurrences/Concurrences": *When a man dies, his secrets bond like crystals, like frost on a window. His last breath obscures the glass* is from Anne Michael's novel *Fugitive Pieces.*

"Sugar Eggs": Max Picard's *The World of Silence* was consulted, as was *Faberge Eggs: Masterpieces from Czarist Russia* by Sussana Pfeffer, for historical material on Faberge eggs.

"The Space Between": quoted material is from *By the Shores of Silver Lake,* by Laura Ingalls Wilder, and Max Picard's, *The World of Silence.*

"Glaciology": Italicized geographical material is from *A Geomorphical Study of Post-Glacial Uplift,* by J. T. Andrews.

THE AUTHOR

Lia Purpura is the author of *Increase* (essays), *Stone Sky Lifting* (poems), *The Brighter the Veil* (poems), and *Poems of Grzegorz Musial: Berliner Tagebuch and Taste of Ash* (translations). Her awards include a National Endowment for the Arts Fellowship in Prose, a Pushcart Prize, a Fulbright Fellowship, the Associated Writing Programs Award in Creative Nonfiction, and the Ohio State University Press / *The Journal* Award in Poetry. Her poems and essays have appeared in *Agni Magazine, DoubleTake, The Georgia Review, The Iowa Review, Parnassus: Poetry in Review, Ploughshares*, and elsewhere. She is Writer-in-Residence at Loyola College in Baltimore, Maryland, and teaches at the Rainier Writing Workshop MFA Program in Tacoma, Washington.